THE

CIRCLES OF LEARNING

COOPERATION IN THE CLASSROOM AND SCHOOL

DAVID W. JOHNSON - ROGER T. JOHNSON - EDYTHE JOHNSON HOLUBEC

ASCD

ASSOCIATION FOR SUPERVISION AND CURRICULUM DEVELOPMENT
ALEXANDRIA, VIRGINIA

Copyright © 1994 by the Association for Supervision and Curriculum
  Development
1250 N. Pitt St.
Alexandria, VA 22314
(703) 549-9110

ASCD publications present a variety of viewpoints. The views expressed or
implied in this publication should not be interpreted as official positions of the
Association.

Printed in the United States of America.

Ronald S. Brandt, *Executive Editor*
Nancy Modrak, *Managing Editor, Books*
Ginger R. Miller, *Associate Editor*
Gary Bloom, *Manager, Design and Production Services*
Karen Monaco, *Senior Graphic Designer*
Valerie Sprague, *Desktop Typesetter*

Price: $13.95
ASCD Stock Number: 1-94034
ISBN: 0-87120-227-1

Library of Congress Cataloging-in-Publication Data

Johnson, David W., 1940–
    The new circles of learning : cooperatin in the classroom and school /
  David W. Johnson, Roger T. Johnson, Edythe Johnson Holubec.
        p.   cm.
    Includes bibliographical references.
    ISBN 0-87120-227-1
    1. Group work in education.   2. Cooperation—Study and teaching.
  I. Johnson, Roger T., 1938–   . II. Holubec, Edythe Johnson.
  III. Title.
  LB1032.J596   1994
  371.3′95—dc20   94-8306
                                                                        CIP

The *New* Circles of Learning: Cooperation in the Classroom and School

David W. Johnson is a Professor of Educational Psychology, and Roger T. Johnson is Professor of Curriculum and Instruction; both are Co-Directors of the Cooperative Learning Center, University of Minnesota, Minneapolis. Edythe Johnson Holubec is a private consultant in Taylor, Texas.

Dedication

This book is dedicated to our parents, Roger and Frances Johnson, who discouraged inappropriate competition and taught us to cooperate.

Acknowledgments

Thanks are due to the thousands of teachers who have carefully structured cooperative learning into the majority of their lessons to create a learning community in which students care about each other and each other's academic progress. They have taught us a lot over the years.

1

What Is Cooperative Learning?

On July 15, 1982, Don Bennett, a Seattle businessman, became the first amputee ever to climb Mount Rainier (reported in Kouzes and Posner 1987). He climbed 14,410 feet on one leg and two crutches. It took him five days. When asked to state the most important lesson he learned from doing the climb, Bennett said without hesitation, "You can't do it alone."

The lesson learned by Bennett is one that we should all take to heart. If classrooms and schools are to become places where people achieve worthy goals, they must become places where students, teachers, administrators, and other staff cooperate in pursuit of those goals. Such cooperation must be consciously implemented until it becomes a natural way of acting and interacting. And it must take place at all levels of schooling from the classroom to the school to the district.

Cooperation in the Classroom

In every classroom, no matter what the subject area, teachers can structure lessons so that students:

1. Engage in a win-lose struggle to see who is best (competition);

2. Work independently on their own learning goals at their own pace and in their own space to achieve a preset criterion of excellence (individualism); or

3. Work cooperatively in small groups, ensuring that all members master the assigned material (cooperation).

Competition

When students are required to *compete* with each other for grades, they work against each other to achieve a goal that only one or a few students can attain. Students are graded on a norm-referenced basis, which requires them to work faster and more accurately than their peers. In doing so, they strive to be better than classmates; work to deprive others (*My winning means you lose.*); celebrate classmates' failures (*Your failure makes it easier for me to win.*); view resources such as grades as limited (*Only a few of us will get "A's."*); recognize their negatively linked fate (*The more you gain, the less there is for me.*); and believe that the most competent and hard-working individuals become "haves" and the less competent and deserving individuals become "have nots" (*Only the strong succeed.*).

In competitive situations there is a negative interdependence among goal achievements; students perceive that they can obtain their goals if and only if the other students in the class fail to obtain theirs (Deutsch 1962; Johnson and Johnson 1991). Unfortunately, this is how most of today's students perceive school. Students either work hard to do better than their classmates, or take it easy because they don't believe they have a chance to win.

Individualism

When students are required to work *individualistically* they work by themselves to accomplish learning goals unrelated to those of the other students. Individual goals are assigned and students' efforts are evaluated on a criteria-referenced basis. Each student has his own set of materials and works at his own speed, ignoring the other students in the class. Students are expected and encouraged to focus on their strict self-interest (*How well can I do?*); value only their own efforts and success (*If I study hard, I may get a high grade.*); and view the success or failure of others as irrelevant (*Whether my classmates study or not does not affect me.*). In such situations, students' goal attainments are independent; students perceive that the achievement of their learning goals is unrelated to what other students do (Deutsch 1962; Johnson and Johnson 1991).

Cooperation

Cooperation means working together to accomplish shared goals. Within cooperative activities individuals seek outcomes that are beneficial to themselves *and* beneficial to all other group members. Cooperative learning is the instructional use of small groups that allows students to work together to maximize their own and each other's learning. The idea is simple. Class members are split into small groups after receiving instruction from the teacher. They then work through the assignment until all group members have successfully understood and completed it. Cooperative efforts result in students striving for mutual benefit so that all group members benefit from each other's efforts (*Your success benefits me and my success benefits you.*); recognizing that all group members share a common fate (*We all sink or swim together here.*); knowing that one's performance is mutually caused by oneself and one's colleagues (*We can't do it without you.*); and feeling proud and jointly celebrating when a group member is recognized for achievement (*You got an A! That's terrific!*). In cooperative learning situations, there is a positive interdependence among students' goal attainments; students perceive that they can reach their learning goals if and only if the other students in the learning group also reach their goals (Deutsch 1962; Johnson and Johnson 1991).

In the ideal classroom, all students would learn how to work collaboratively with others, compete for fun and enjoyment, and work autonomously on their own. Teachers must decide which goal structure to implement within each lesson. This book is designed to provide an understanding of cooperative learning that will enable teachers to create lessons based on cooperation in the classroom and improve current efforts to structure lessons cooperatively while also exploring the importance of cooperation at all levels of the school.

Essential Components:
What Makes Cooperation Work

Together we stand, divided we fall.
Watchword of
the American Revolution

In order to achieve real expertise in using cooperative learning, you must first understand what cooperative learning is (see Figure 1.1).

FIGURE 1.1

Circles of Learning

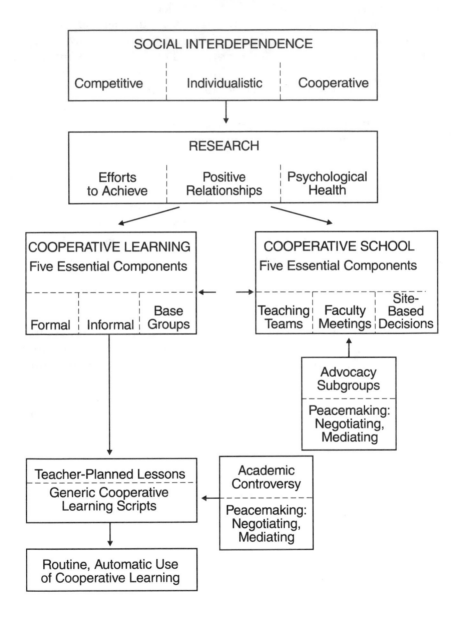

Understanding cooperation includes understanding the five essential components that make cooperation work (see Chapter 3). Educators must then know how to plan and implement formal cooperative learning lessons (see Chapter 4), informal cooperative learning lessons (see Chapter 5), cooperative base groups (see Chapter 6), and cooperative learning scripts or structures for repetitive lessons and classroom routines (see Chapter 4, page 43). Once you plan, structure, and implement hundreds of cooperative learning lessons, you will achieve a routine-level of implementation and you will be able to integrate the various forms of cooperative learning (see Chapter 7). In order to get to this level, it will be necessary for students to learn cooperative skills (see Chapter 8), which includes handling conflict (see Chapter 9). Implementation of cooperative learning, furthermore, takes place within an organizational context, which ideally is the cooperative school (see Chapter 10).

Clearly, there is more to cooperative learning than a seating arrangement. Placing students in groups and telling them to work together does not in and of itself result in cooperative efforts. Sitting in groups can instead result in competition at close quarters or individualistic efforts with talking. To structure lessons so students do in fact work cooperatively with each other requires an understanding of the components that make cooperation work. Mastering the essential components of cooperation allows teachers to:

1. Take existing lessons, curriculums, and courses and structure them cooperatively;

2. Tailor cooperative learning lessons to unique instructional needs, circumstances, curriculums, subject areas, and students; and

3. Diagnose the problems some students might have working together and intervene to increase the effectiveness of student learning groups.

For cooperation to work well, teachers must explicitly structure five essential components within each lesson (see Chapter 3). The first and most important component is *positive interdependence*. Positive interdependence is successfully structured when group members perceive that they are linked with each other so that one cannot succeed unless everyone succeeds. Students must realize that each member's efforts benefit not only the individual, but all other group members as well. Students' vested interest in each other's achievement results in their sharing resources, helping and assisting each other's efforts to learn, providing mutual support, and celebrating their joint success. Positive interdependence is the heart of cooperative learning.

The second essential component of cooperative learning is *promotive interaction*, preferably face-to-face. Once teachers establish positive interdependence, they need to maximize the opportunity for students to promote each other's success by helping, assisting, supporting, encouraging, and praising each other's efforts to learn. There are cognitive activities and interpersonal dynamics that only occur when students get involved in promoting each other's learning. Promotive interaction includes orally explaining how to solve problems, discussing the nature of the concepts being learned, teaching one's knowledge to classmates, and connecting present and past learning.

The third essential component of cooperative learning is *individual accountability*. The purpose of cooperative learning groups is to make each member a stronger individual. Students learn together so they can subsequently perform better as individuals. Individual accountability exists when the performance of each individual student is assessed and the results are given back to the group and the individual. Individual accountability ensures that group members know who needs more assistance, support, and encouragement in completing the assignment and are aware that they cannot "hitch-hike" on the work of others.

The fourth essential component of cooperative learning is *interpersonal and small-group skills*. In cooperative learning groups, students are required to learn academic subject matter (taskwork) as well as the interpersonal and small-group skills required to function as part of a team (teamwork). This makes cooperative learning inherently more complex than competitive or individualistic learning. Placing socially unskilled individuals in a group and telling them to cooperate does not guarantee that they will be able to do so effectively. Skills such as leadership, decision making, trust-building, communication, and conflict management must be taught just as purposefully and precisely as academic skills. There are many successful procedures and strategies for teaching students social skills (See Johnson and Johnson 1991, 1993; and Johnson and F. Johnson 1991).

The fifth essential component of cooperative learning is *group processing*. Group processing exists when group members discuss how well they are achieving their goals and maintaining effective working relationships. Groups need to describe what member actions are helpful and unhelpful and make decisions about what behaviors to continue or change.

Real expertise in using cooperative learning is gained by learning how to structure the five essential components into instructional activities (Johnson and Johnson 1989a). These essential components, further-more, should be carefully structured within all levels of cooperative efforts—learning groups, the class as a whole, the teaching team, the school, and the school district.

Types of Cooperative Learning

Children sit for 12 years in classrooms where the implicit goal is to listen to the teacher and memorize the information in order to regurgitate it on a test. Little or no attention is paid to the learning process, even though much research exists documenting that real understanding is a case of active restructuring on the part of the learner. Restructuring occurs through engagement in problem posing as well as problem solving, inference making and investigation, resolving of contradictions, and reflecting. These processes all man-date far more active learners, as well as a different model of educa-tion than the one subscribed to at present by most institutions. Rather than being powerless and dependent on the institution, learners need to be empowered to think and learn for themselves. Thus, learning needs to be conceived of as something a learner does, not something that is done to a learner.

Catherine Fosnot 1989

Cooperative learning can be used in various ways, including formal cooperative learning, informal cooperative learning, cooperative base groups, and cooperative structures.

Formal Cooperative Learning

Formal cooperative learning is students working together, from one class period to several weeks, to achieve shared learning goals by ensuring that they and their groupmates successfully complete the learning task assigned. As we've stated, any learning task in any subject area with any curriculum can be structured cooperatively. Any course requirement or assignment may be reformulated for formal cooperative learning. In formal cooperative learning groups, teachers (a) specify the objectives for the lesson, (b) make a number of pre-instructional deci-sions, (c) explain the task and the positive interdependence, (d) monitor students' learning and intervene within the groups to provide task assistance or to increase students' interpersonal and group skills, and

(e) evaluate students' learning and help students process how well their groups functioned (see Chapter 4).

Informal Cooperative Learning

Does the use of cooperative learning mean that teachers can no longer lecture, give demonstrations, show films, or use videotapes? No.

Lectures, demonstrations, films, and videotapes may be used effectively with informal cooperative learning groups in which students work together to achieve a joint learning goal in temporary, ad-hoc groups that last from a few minutes to one class period. During a lecture, demonstration, or film, quick informal cooperative groupings can be used to focus student attention on the material to be learned, to set a mood conducive to learning, to help set expectations as to what will be covered in a class session, to ensure that students cognitively process the material being taught, and to provide closure to the instructional session. Informal cooperative learning helps teachers ensure that students do the intellectual work of organizing, explaining, summarizing, and integrating material into existing conceptual structures during direct teaching. Informal cooperative learning groups are often organized so that students engage in a three- to five-minute focused discussion before and after a lecture and two- to three-minute turn-to-your-partner discussions throughout a lecture (see Chapter 5).

Cooperative Base Groups

Are all cooperative learning groups temporary, lasting only for a short period of time? No.

Cooperative base groups are long-term, heterogeneous cooperative learning groups with stable membership that last for at least a year and perhaps until all members are graduated. These groups provide students with permanent, committed relationships that allow group members to give each other the needed support, help, encouragement, and assistance to consistently work hard in school, make academic progress (attend class, complete all assignments, learn), and develop in cognitively and socially healthy ways (Johnson, Johnson, and Holubec 1992; Johnson, Johnson, and Smith 1991).

Base groups meet formally each day in elementary school and twice a week in secondary school (or whenever the class meets). Informally, members interact every day within and between classes, discussing assignments and helping each other with homework. The use of base groups tends to improve attendance, personalize the work required and the school experience, and improve the quality and quantity of learning. The larger the class or school and the more complex and difficult the subject matter, the more important it is to have base groups. Base groups are also helpful in structuring homerooms and when a teacher meets with a number of advisees (see Chapter 6).

Cooperative Structures

In order to use cooperative learning the majority of the time teachers must identify and cooperatively structure generic lessons and repetitive course routines. Cooperative learning scripts are standard, content-free cooperative procedures, which proscribe student actions step-by-step, for either (a) conducting generic, repetitive lessons (such as writing reports or giving presentations) or (b) managing classroom routines (such as checking homework and reviewing tests). Scripted, repetitive cooperative lessons and classroom routines provide a base on which the cooperative classroom can be built. Once planned and conducted several times, they become automatic activities in the classroom. They can also be used in combination to form an overall lesson (see Chapter 4).

As teachers use formal, informal, and cooperative base groups and generic cooperative structures such as learning scripts they gain expertise and begin to automatically use cooperative learning as needed. When teachers achieve the routine-use level of teacher competence they are able to structure cooperative learning situations automatically without conscious thought or planning using various types of cooperative learning. Cooperative learning can then be used long-term with fidelity (see Chapter 7).

Teaching Cooperative Skills

When implementing cooperative learning in the classroom and the school, one major issue becomes, "How well do group members manage conflicts?" Cooperation and conflict go hand-in-hand. The more group members care about achieving the group's goals, and the more they care about each other, the more frequently conflicts will occur. When conflicts are managed constructively, they add creativity, fun, and higher-level reasoning. When they are managed destructively, they can result in anger, frustration, and hostility. In order to manage conflicts constructively, students and faculty need to learn the procedures for doing so and become skillful in their use.

In a conflict positive school (or learning group), members promote and seek out conflicts in order to reap the many positive outcomes they can bring. Two types of conflicts are essential for cooperative groups to function effectively (see Chapter 9). The first type is academic controversy in which students challenge each other's intellectual reasoning and conclusions and argue the different sides of an issue (Johnson and Johnson 1992). The second is peer mediation in which all students are taught how to negotiate solutions to their conflicts with schoolmates and faculty and how to mediate conflicts among their peers (Johnson and Johnson 1991). When conflicts are managed constructively within a group, class, and school, the stage is set for cooperative learning and the cooperative school to reach their potential.

The Cooperative School

All of the elements and benefits of cooperative learning in the classroom must be applied and reflected in the school as a whole (see Chapter 10). The current context of schooling is a "mass-production" organizational structure that divides work into small component parts performed by individuals separately from and in competition with peers. The alternative context is a team-based, high-performance organizational structure in which individuals work cooperatively in teams that have responsibility for an entire product, process, or set of customers. The new organizational structure is known as "the cooperative school."

In a cooperative school, students work primarily in cooperative learning groups and teachers and building staff as well as district administrators work in cooperative teams (Johnson and Johnson 1989b). The organizational structure of the classroom, school, and district are thus congruent. Each level of cooperative teams supports and enhances the other levels.

Implementing Cooperation in the School

The cooperative school begins in the classroom. Students spend the majority of the day in cooperative learning groups. Cooperative learning is used to increase student achievement, create more positive relationships among students, and generally improve students' psychological well-being. What is good for students, furthermore, is even better for faculty.

The second level of the cooperative school is for faculty to work in collegial support groups aimed at increasing their instructional expertise and success. Faculty work teams are just as effective as student work teams. The use of cooperation to structure faculty and staff work involves (a) collegial support groups, (b) school-based decision making, and (c) faculty meetings. Just as the heart of the classroom is cooperative learning, the heart of the school is the collegial support group. School-based decision making is implemented through the use of two types of cooperative teams. First, a *task force* considers a school problem and proposes a solution to the faculty as a whole. Second, the faculty is divided into *ad hoc decision-making groups*, which consider whether to accept or modify the proposal. The decisions made by the ad hoc groups are summarized, and the entire faculty then decides on the action to be taken to solve the problem. The use of faculty collegial support groups, task forces, and ad hoc decision-making groups tends to increase teacher productivity, cohesion, and professional self-esteem. Faculty meetings, furthermore, become models of cooperative procedures.

The third level of the cooperative school is at the district level where administrators are organized into *collegial support groups* to increase their administrative expertise and success. Administrative task forces and ad hoc decision-making groups should dominate decision making at the district level as much as at the school level. District-level educators must remember that cooperation is more than an instructional procedure. It is a basic shift in organizational structure that extends from the classroom through the superintendent's office.

Gaining Expertise In Using Cooperative Learning

Knowledge about how to do something is not a skill. Being able to do something well is a skill. Skills take considerable time and effort to develop. Gaining expertise in using cooperative learning in the classroom and cooperative teams in the school and district takes at least one lifetime. *Expertise* is reflected in a person's proficiency, adroitness, competence, and skill in structuring cooperative efforts. Expertise, furthermore, focuses attention on the transfer of what is learned within training sessions to the workplace and the long-term maintenance of new procedures throughout a person's career and lifetime.

James Watson, who won a Nobel Prize as the codiscoverer of the double helix, stated, "Nothing new that is really interesting comes without collaboration." Gaining expertise in using cooperative learning is in itself a cooperative process that requires a team effort. Collegial support groups encourage and assist teachers in a long-term, multi-year effort to continually improve their competence in using cooperative learning (Johnson and Johnson 1989b). With only a moderately difficult teaching strategy, for example, teachers may require from 20 to 30 hours of instruction in its theory, 15 to 20 demonstrations using it with different students and subjects, and an additional 10 to 15 coaching sessions to attain higher-level skills. For a more difficult teaching strategy like cooperative learning, several years of training and support may be needed to ensure mastery.

As Aristotle said, "For things we have to learn before we can do them, we learn by doing them." Teachers have to do cooperative learning for some time before they begin to gain real expertise. This requires support, encouragement, and assistance from colleagues. Transfer and maintenance, therefore, depend largely on teachers themselves being organized into cooperative teams (collegial support groups) that focus on helping each member progressively improve their competence in using cooperative learning. For teachers to be organized this way and to organize their classes this way, administrators and district-level staff must also be organized cooperatively and model cooperation.

Throughout one very difficult trek across an ice field during Don Bennett's hop to the top of Mount Rainier, his daughter stayed by his side for four hours and with each new hop told him, "You can do it, Dad. You're the best dad in the world. You can do it, Dad." There was no way Bennett would quit hopping with his daughter yelling words of love and encouragement in his ear. The encouragement of his daughter kept him going, strengthening his commitment to make it to the top. Likewise, with members of cooperative groups cheering them on, students and educators amaze themselves with what they can achieve.

2

Research on
Cooperative Learning

---

*Two are better than one, because they have a good reward for toil.
For if they fall, one will lift up his fellow; but woe to him who is alone
when he falls and has not another to lift him up . . . And though a
man might prevail against one who is alone, two will withstand him.
A threefold cord is not quickly broken.*
                                                    —Ecclesiastes 4:9-12

Where We've Been: Theoretical Roots

Cooperative learning has a rich history of theory, research, and actual
classroom use, which makes it one of the most distinguished of all
instructional practices. At least three general theoretical perspectives—
social interdependence theory, cognitive developmental theory, and
behavioral learning theory—have guided research on cooperative learning.

Social Interdependence Theory

Perhaps the most influential theorizing on cooperative learning
focuses on *social interdependence*. In the early 1900s, one of the foun-
ders of the gestalt school of psychology, Kurt Kafka, proposed that groups
were dynamic wholes in which the interdependence among members
varied. One of his colleagues, Kurt Lewin (1935, 1948), refined Kafka's

notions in the 1920s and 1930s. According to Lewin, the essence of a group is the interdependence among members (created by common goals) that results in the group being a "dynamic whole." A change in the state of any member or subgroup changes the state of any other member or subgroup; an intrinsic state of tension among group members motivates their movement toward accomplishing the desired common goals. One of Lewin's graduate students, Morton Deutsch (1949a, 1962), in the late 1940s formulated a theory of cooperation and competition, which we have extended into the *social interdependence theory* (Johnson and Johnson 1974, 1989a).

The social interdependence perspective assumes that the way social interdependence is structured determines how individuals interact, which, in turn, determines outcomes (Johnson and Johnson 1974, 1989a). Positive interdependence (cooperation) results in promotive interaction as individuals encourage and facilitate each other's efforts. Negative interdependence (competition) typically results in oppositional interaction as individuals discourage and obstruct each other's efforts to achieve. In the absence of interdependence (individualistic efforts) there is no interaction as individuals work independently.

Cognitive Developmental Theory

The *cognitive developmental perspective* is largely based on the work of Piaget, Vygotsky, and related theorists. Piaget espoused the premise that when individuals cooperate on the environment, socio-cognitive conflict occurs that creates cognitive disequilibrium, which in turn stimulates their perspective-taking ability and cognitive development. Piagetians argue that during cooperative efforts, participants engage in discussions in which cognitive conflicts occur and are resolved, and inadequate reasoning is exposed and modified. Similarly, the work of Vygotsky is based on the premise that knowledge is social, and is constructed from cooperative efforts to learn, understand, and solve problems. Group members exchange information and insights, discover weak points in each other's reasoning strategies, correct one another, and adjust their understandings on the basis of one another's understandings.

Related to developmental theorists are the controversy theorists (Johnson and Johnson 1979, 1992a) and the cognitive restructuring theorists. Controversy theorists posit that being confronted with opposing points of view creates uncertainty, or conceptual conflict, which, in turn, creates a reconceptualization and an information search that results in a more refined and thoughtful conclusion. Cognitive restructuring theorists believe that in order for information to be retained in memory and incorporated into existing cognitive structures, the learner must cognitively rehearse and restructure the material by, for example, explaining the material to a collaborator (Wittrock 1990).

Behavioral Learning Theory

The *behavioral learning theory* perspective focuses on the impact of group reinforcers and rewards on learning. The assumption is that actions followed by extrinsic rewards are repeated. Skinner focused on group contingencies, Bandura focused on imitation, and Homans and Thibaut and Kelley focused on the balance of rewards and costs in social exchange among interdependent individuals. More recently, Slavin (1980) has emphasized the need for extrinsic group rewards to motivate people to learn in cooperative learning groups.

There are basic differences among the three theoretical perspectives. Social interdependence theory assumes that cooperative efforts are based on intrinsic motivation generated by interpersonal factors associated with working together and joint aspirations to achieve a significant goal. Social interdependence theory is made up of relational concepts dealing with what happens among individuals (e.g., cooperation is something that exists only among individuals, not within them), while cognitive developmental theory is focused on what happens within a single person (e.g., disequilibrium, cognitive reorganization). Behavioral-social theory assumes that cooperative efforts are powered by extrinsic motivation to achieve group rewards. The differences in basic assumptions among the three theoretical perspectives create theoretical conflicts and disagreements that have yet to be fully explored or resolved. Theorists concerned with these three theoretical perspectives have, however, generated a considerable body of research to confirm or disprove many of their predictions.

Where We've Been: Research

We've known a lot about cooperation for quite some time. Since 1898, over 550 experimental and 100 correlational research studies have been conducted on cooperative, competitive, and individualistic efforts (see Johnson and Johnson 1989 for a complete review of these studies).

Around the turn of the century, Triplett in the United States, Turner in England, and Mayer in Germany conducted a series of studies on the factors associated with competitive performance. Since then, much research about cooperation has been conducted and disseminated. In 1929, Maller wrote a book about it, as did May and Doob in 1937. In 1949, Deutsch published a research review and a theory on cooperation. In 1963, Miller and Hamblin reviewed 24 studies on it. In 1970 and 1974, we published comprehensive research reviews. Since 1974, the research review articles have been too numerous to mention, but they have clearly proven several things about the importance of cooperation during learning efforts.

The effectiveness of cooperative learning has been confirmed by both theoretical and demonstration research, and the literature includes both "scientific" literature and "professional" literature. The scientific literature is made up of carefully controlled research studies conducted to validate or disconfirm theory. Most of the studies are either laboratory or field experimental studies. The professional literature consists of field quasi-experimental or correlational studies demonstrating that cooperative learning works in real classrooms for a prolonged period of time. The demonstration studies are grouped into (1) summative evaluations demonstrating that cooperative learning produces beneficial results; (2) comparative summative evaluations demonstrating that one cooperative learning procedure works better than others; (3) formative evaluations aimed at improving ongoing implementations of cooperative learning; and (4) survey studies on the impact of cooperative learning on students (Johnson and Johnson 1994).

Cooperative learning can be used with some confidence at every grade level, in every subject area, and with any task. Research on cooperation learning has included participants who vary with regard to economic class, age, sex, nationality, and cultural background. A wide variety of research tasks, ways of structuring cooperation, and measures of the dependent variables have been used. The studies have been conducted by many different researchers with markedly different orientations working in different settings and countries during different decades. As a result, the research on cooperative learning has a validity and a generalizability rarely found in education literature.

Cooperation is a generic human endeavor that affects many different instructional outcomes simultaneously. Over the past 90 years, researchers have focused on such diverse outcomes as achievement, higher-level reasoning, retention, motivation, transfer of learning, interpersonal attraction, friendships, prejudice, valuing differences, social support, self-esteem, social competencies, psychological health, and moral reasoning. These numerous outcomes may be subsumed within three broad categories (Johnson and Johnson 1989a): effort to achieve, positive interpersonal relationships, and psychological health (see Figure 2.1).

FIGURE 2.1

Outcomes of Cooperation

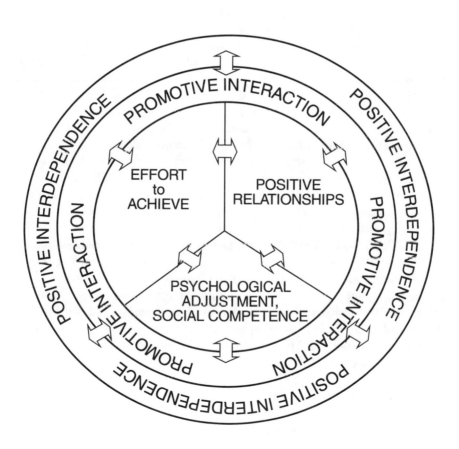

History of Practical Use of Cooperative Learning

Cooperative learning has a rich and long history of practical use. Thousands of years ago the Talmud stated that in order to understand its contents, each reader must have a learning partner. As early as the 1st century, Quintillion argued that students could benefit from teaching one another. The Roman philosopher, Seneca, advocated cooperative learning through such statements as, "Qui Docet Discet" ("When you teach, you learn twice"). And Johann Amos Comenius (1592-1679) believed that students would benefit both by teaching and being taught by other students.

In the late 1700s, Joseph Lancaster and Andrew Bell made extensive use of cooperative learning groups in England, and the idea was brought to America when a Lancastrian school opened in New York City in 1806. In the United States in the early 1800s, the Common School Movement also placed a strong emphasis on cooperative learning. In fact, during many periods, cooperative learning has been widely advocated and used to promote educational goals.

One of the most successful advocates of cooperative learning in America was Colonel Francis Parker. In the last three decades of the 19th century, Colonel Parker brought to his advocacy of cooperative learning enthusiasm, idealism, practicality, and an intense devotion to freedom, democracy, and individuality in the public schools. His fame and success rested on the vivid and regenerating spirit that he brought into the schoolroom and on his power to create a classroom atmosphere that was truly cooperative and democratic. When he was superintendent of the public schools in Quincy, Massachusetts (1875-1880), more than 30,000 people a year visited to examine his use of cooperative learning procedures (Campbell 1965). Parker's instructional methods of structuring cooperation among students dominated American education through the turn of the century. Following Parker, John Dewey (1924) promoted the use of cooperative learning groups as part of his famous project method in instruction. The late 1930s, however, saw the beginnings of interpersonal competition emphasized in public schools (Pepitone 1980).

In the mid-1960s we began training teachers in the use of cooperative learning at the University of Minnesota. The Cooperative Learning Center was formed as a result of our efforts to:

- synthesize existing knowledge concerning cooperative, competitive, and individualistic efforts (Johnson 1970, Johnson and Johnson 1974, 1978, 1983, 1989);
- formulate theoretical models concerning the nature of cooperation and its essential components;
- conduct a systematic program of research to test our theories;
- translate the validated theory into a set of concrete strategies and procedures for using cooperation in classrooms, schools, and school districts (Johnson, Johnson, and Holubec 1993, Johnson and Johnson 1975/1994); and
- build and maintain a network of schools and colleges implementing cooperative strategies and procedures throughout North America and in a variety of other countries around the world.

In the early 1970s, David DeVries and Keith Edwards at Johns Hopkins University developed Teams-Games-Tournaments (TGT) and Sholmo and Yael Sharan in Israel developed the group investigation procedure for cooperative learning groups. In the late 1970s, Robert Slavin extended DeVries and Edwards' work by modifying TGT into Student-Team-Achievement-Divisions (STAD) and modifying computer-assisted instruction into Team-Assisted Instruction (TAI). Concurrently, Spencer Kagan developed the Co-op Co-op procedure. And in the 1980s, Donald Dansereau developed a number of cooperative procedures, which he calls scripts.

Outcomes of Cooperation

In *Look Homeward Angel*, Thomas Wolfe tells about how Eugene was taught to write by a grammar school classmate, learning from a peer what "all instruction failed" to teach him. Is Eugene the only one? In trying to find out, several questions have to be answered about the impact of cooperative learning. The first is, "What is the conclusion when all the available studies are included in the analysis?" Over 375 experimental studies on achievement have been conducted over the past 90 years (Johnson and Johnson 1989). A meta-analysis of all studies indicates that cooperative learning results in significantly higher achievement and retention than do competitive and individualistic learning (see Figure 2.2 on page 20).

FIGURE 2.2

Meta-Analysis of Research on Social Interdependence

	mean	s.d.	n
Achievement			
Cooperative vs. Competitive	0.67	0.93	129
Cooperative vs. Individualistic	0.64	0.79	184
Competitive vs. Individualistic	0.30	0.77	38
Interpersonal Attraction			
Cooperative vs. Competitive	0.67	0.49	93
Cooperative vs. Individualistic	0.60	0.58	60
Competitive vs. Individualistic	0.08	0.70	15
Social Support			
Cooperative vs. Competitive	0.62	0.44	84
Cooperative vs. Individualistic	0.70	0.45	72
Competitive vs. Individualistic	-0.13	0.36	19
Self-Esteem			
Cooperative vs. Competitive	0.58	0.56	56
Cooperative vs. Individualistic	0.44	0.40	38
Competitive vs. Individualistic	-0.23	0.42	19

Reprinted with permission from D.W. Johnson and R. Johnson (1989). *Cooperation and Competition: Theory and Research.* Edina, Minn.: Interaction Book Company.

The second question is, "What is the conclusion when only the methodological high-quality studies are analyzed?" The superiority of cooperative over competitive or individualistic efforts is still pronounced.

The third question is, "What is the conclusion when the results of studies that used 'pure' operationalizations of cooperation are compared with the results of studies that used 'mixed' operationalizations of cooperation?" Some cooperative learning procedures contain a mixture of cooperative, competitive, and individualistic efforts, while others contain pure cooperation. The original Jigsaw procedure (Aronson 1978), for example, is a combination of resource interdependence and an individualistic reward structure. Teams-Games-Tournaments and Student-Teams-Achievement-Divisions are mixtures of cooperation and intergroup competition. Team-Assisted-Instruction (Slavin, Leavey, and Madden 1982) is a mixture of individualistic and cooperative learning. When the results of "pure" and "mixed" operationalizations of cooperative learning are compared, the pure operationalizations show the highest achievement (effect sizes: cooperative vs. competitive, pure = 0.71, mixed = 0.40; cooperative vs. individualistic, pure = 65, mixed = 0.42).

Cooperative, compared with competitive or individualistic efforts, furthermore, tend to result in more higher-level reasoning, more frequent creation of new ideas and solutions (i.e., process gain), and greater transfer of what is learned within one situation to another (i.e., group to individual transfer) (see Johnson and Johnson 1989).

Within cooperative learning groups there is a process of interpersonal exchange that promotes the use of higher-level thinking strategies, higher-level reasoning, and metacognitive strategies. Students working together cooperatively expect to, and do in fact, explain what they learn to groupmates, elaborate on what is being learned, listen to others' perspectives and ideas, monitor each other's participation and contributions, give each other feedback, and engage in intellectual conflict.

Kurt Lewin often said, "I always found myself unable to think as a single person." Learning is a personal and social process that results when individuals cooperate to construct shared understandings and knowledge. Competitive and individualistic structures, by isolating students from each other, tend to suppress achievement. Therefore, when teachers want to maximize students' learning, increase their retention, and promote the use of higher-level reasoning strategies, they would be well advised to use cooperative rather than competitive or individualistic methods.

Interpersonal Relationships and Social Support

Vince Lombardi, the famous coach of the Green Bay Packers, once said, "Heartpower is the strength of your corporation." Learning communities are based as much on relationships as they are on intellectual discourse. Love of learning and love of each other inspire students to commit more and more of their energy to their studies because long-term, dedicated efforts to achieve come from the heart, not the head. Within any classroom, teachers must reach students' hearts if students are to exert extraordinary efforts to learn, and peer relationships are the key to reaching students' hearts.

Since the 1940s, 106 studies have compared the relative impact of cooperative, competitive, and individualistic efforts on social support. Cooperative experiences promote greater social support than do competitive or individualistic experiences. This is important, as social support promotes achievement and productivity, physical health, psychological health, and the ability to cope with stress and adversity.

The more students care about each other and the more committed they are to each other's success, the harder each student will work and the more productive each will be. As relationships become more positive, absenteeism and dropout rates decrease, while commitment to educational goals, feelings of personal responsibility to the school, willingness to take on difficult tasks, motivation and persistence in working toward goal achievement, satisfaction, morale, acceptance of pain and frustration as part of learning, desire to listen to and be influenced by classmates and teachers, and commitment to each other's learning and success increase (Johnson and F. Johnson 1994; Johnson and Johnson 1989). Thus, to maximize student learning, teachers need to promote caring and committed relationships among classmates.

Individuals care more about each other and are more committed to each other's success and well-being when they work together cooperatively than when they compete to see who is best or work independently from each other. The more often students learn in cooperative groups, the more they like each other. This is true when individuals are homogeneous as well as when individuals differ in intellectual ability, handicapping conditions, ethnic membership, social class, and gender. Relationships are built on interdependence (Johnson 1993). In fact, cooperative learning has proven to be an essential prerequisite for managing diversity within the classroom. When individuals cooperate with each other, the positive interdependence and promotive interaction result in students' frequent and accurate communication, accurate perspective-taking, inducibility, development of multidimensional views of others, feelings of psychological acceptance and self-esteem, psychological success, and expectations of rewarding and productive future interaction (Johnson and Johnson 1989a).

Psychological Adjustment

Asley Montagu was fond of saying, "With few exceptions, the solitary animal is, in any species, an abnormal creature." Karen Horney said,

"The neurotic individual is someone who is inappropriately competitive and, therefore, unable to cooperate with others." Montagu and Horney recognized that the essence of psychological health is the ability to develop and maintain cooperative relationships. Working cooperatively with peers, and valuing cooperation, results in greater psychological health (and greater social competencies and higher self-esteem) than competing with peers or working independently. Students' psychological health is best in schools dominated by cooperative efforts. The more individuals work cooperatively with others, the more they see themselves as worthwhile and valuable; develop social competencies; form caring, supportive personal relationships; and successfully cope with adversity. Personal ego-strength, self-confidence, independence, and autonomy are all promoted through involvement in cooperative groups. Cooperative experiences in schools are not a luxury. They are an absolute necessity for the healthy development of students who can function independently.

Since the 1950s, over 80 studies have compared the relative impact of cooperative, competitive, and individualistic experiences on self-esteem. Research demonstrates that cooperative experiences help students believe they are intrinsically worthwhile and viewed by others in positive ways, compare their personal attributes favorably with those of their peers, and judge themselves to be capable, competent, and successful. This is because in cooperative efforts, students (1) realize that they are accurately known, accepted, and liked by peers, (2) know they contribute to their own, others', and the group's success, and (3) perceive themselves and others in a differentiated and realistic way that allows for multidimensional comparisons based on complementarity of individuals' abilities. Competitive experiences tend to be related to conditional self-esteem based on whether one wins or loses. Individualistic experiences tend to be related to basic self-rejection.

Everything Affects Everything Else

Each of the outcomes of cooperative efforts—achievement, quality of relationships, and psychological health—influences the others (see Figure 2.1 on page 17) (Johnson and Johnson 1989a). First, caring and committed friendships come from a sense of mutual accomplishment, mutual pride in joint work, and the bonding that results from joint efforts. The more students care about each other, the harder they work to achieve mutual learning goals. Second, joint efforts to achieve mutual goals promote higher self-esteem, self-efficacy, personal control, and self-confidence. Conversely, the psychologically healthier individuals are, the better able they are to work with others to achieve mutual goals. Third, psychological health is built on the internalization of the caring and respect received from others. Friendships are developmental advantages that promote self-esteem, self-efficacy, and general positive psychological adjustment. Psychologically healthy people (people who are free of depression, paranoia, anxiety, fear of failure, repressed anger, hopelessness, and meaninglessness) are able to maintain caring, committed relationships. Thus, the outcomes of cooperative efforts are a package, with each outcome serving as a door into the others.

Group efforts can go wrong in many ways. Much of our research over the past 25 years has focused on identifying what makes cooperation work. The powerful impact of genuine cooperative efforts on achievement, retention, higher-level reasoning, creative generation of new ideas, and transfer of learning is apparent in the overall evidence. Confidence in these results is increased by the fact that the results of high-quality studies are similar, and studies using pure cooperation show greater achievement than studies using mixtures of cooperative, competitive, and individualistic efforts. If we as educators are to implement cooperative learning successfully, we must understand its essential components, which are the focus of the next chapter.

3

Essential Components of Cooperative Learning

Coming together is a beginning; keeping together is progress; working together is success.

—Henry Ford

Cooperation Is More Than a Seating Arrangement

Structuring cooperative learning involves more than seating a number of students close together and telling them to help each other. Many actions can hurt group efforts. Less able members sometimes "leave it to George" to complete the group's tasks, thus creating a free rider effect (Kerr and Bruun 1981) whereby group members expend decreasing amounts of effort and just go through the motions of teamwork. At the same time, "George" may expend less effort to avoid the sucker effect of doing all the work (Kerr 1983). While working in a group, students might also defer to high-ability group members, who may take over the important leadership roles in ways that benefit them at the expense of the rest of the group (the rich-get-richer effect). For example, a high-ability group member may give all the explanations of what is being learned. Because the amount of time spent explaining correlates highly with the amount learned, the more able member learns a great deal while less able members flounder as a captive audience. Group efforts can also be characterized by self-induced helplessness (Langer and Benevento

1978), diffusion of responsibility and social loafing (Latane, Williams, and Harkin 1979), reactance (Salomon 1981), dysfunctional divisions of labor ("I'm the thinkist and you're the typist") (Sheingold, Hawkins, and Char 1984), inappropriate dependence on authority (Webb, Ender, and Lewis 1986), destructive conflict (Collins 1970, Johnson and Johnson 1979), ganging up against a task, and other patterns of behavior that debilitate group performance.

Cooperation often goes wrong due to the absence of certain conditions that mediate its effectiveness. These conditions are the essential components that make cooperative efforts more productive than competitive and individualistic efforts. These essential components are:

- Clearly perceived positive interdependence
- Considerable promotive (face-to-face) interaction
- Clearly perceived individual accountability and personal responsibility to achieve the group's goals
- Frequent use of relevant interpersonal and small-group skills
- Frequent and regular group processing of current functioning to improve future effectiveness.

FIGURE 3.1

Essential Components of Cooperative Learning

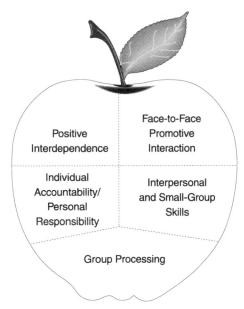

Positive Interdependence: "We Instead of Me"

All for one and one for all.
—Alexandre Dumas

In football, the quarterback who throws the pass and the receiver who catches the pass are positively interdependent. The success of one depends on the success of the other. Their mutual success depends on each of them performing competently. Likewise, the first requirement for an effectively structured cooperative lesson is that students believe that they "sink or swim together." Within cooperative learning situations students have two responsibilities: to learn the assigned material and to ensure that all members of their group learn it. The technical term for this dual responsibility is *positive interdependence*. Positive interdependence exists when students perceive that they are linked with groupmates in a way that makes it impossible for anyone to succeed unless the entire group succeeds (and vice versa) and that they must coordinate their efforts with their groupmates to complete a task.

Positive interdependence promotes a situation in which students (1) see that their work benefits groupmates and that groupmates' work benefits them and (2) work together in small groups to maximize the learning of all members by sharing their resources, providing mutual support and encouragement, and celebrating their joint success. When positive interdependence is clearly established, it highlights the fact that:

• Each group member's efforts are required and indispensable for group success (i.e., there can be no "free riders"); and
• Each group member has a unique contribution to make to the joint effort because of his resources, role, and task responsibilities.

Structuring Positive Interdependence

Positive interdependence can be structured four ways within a learning group, through:

Positive Goal Interdependence: Students perceive that they can achieve their learning goals only if *all* group members attain their goals. To ensure that students believe this and care about how much each other learns, a teacher must structure a clear group or mutual goal such as "learn the assigned material and make sure that all members of your group learn it." The group goal must always be a part of the lesson.

Positive Reward/Celebration Interdependence: Each group member receives the same reward when the group achieves its goals. To supplement goal interdependence, teachers can add joint rewards (e.g., if all members of the group get 90 percent correct or better on the test, each will receive five bonus points). Sometimes teachers give students a group grade for the overall production of their group, individual grades from tests, and bonus points if all group members achieve up to the criterion on the tests. Regular celebrations of group efforts and success enhance the quality of cooperation.

Positive Resource Interdependence: Each group member has only a portion of the resources, information, or materials necessary to complete the given task. Therefore, members must pool their resources to achieve their goals. Teachers may wish to highlight cooperative relationships by giving students limited resources that must be shared (one copy of the problem or task per group) or giving each student part of the required resources that the group must then fit together (the Jigsaw procedure).

Positive Role Interdependence: Each member is assigned complementary and interconnected roles that specify responsibilities required for the group to complete the joint task. Teachers create role interdependence among students by assigning them complementary roles such as reader, recorder, checker of understanding, encourager of participation, and elaborator of knowledge (see Chapter 8). Such roles are vital to high-quality learning.

Other types of positive interdependence can also be structured into lessons. *Positive task interdependence* involves creating a division of labor so that the actions of one group member have to be completed in order for the next member to complete her responsibility. In *positive identity interdependence,* a mutual identity is established through use of a name or motto. Placing groups in competition with each other creates *outside enemy interdependence.* And *fantasy interdependence* results when group members are given a task that requires them to imagine they're in a hypothetical situation.

We have conducted a series of studies investigating the nature of positive interdependence and the relative power of the different types of positive interdependence (Hwong, Caswell, Johnson, and Johnson in press; Johnson, Johnson, Stanne, and Garibaldi 1990; Johnson, Johnson, Ortiz, and Stanne 1991; Lew, Mesch, Johnson, and Johnson 1986a, 1986b; Mesch, Johnson, and Johnson 1988; Mesch, Lew, Johnson, and Johnson

1986). We have concluded that positive interdependence provides the context within which promotive interaction occurs; that group membership and interpersonal interaction among students don't produce higher achievement unless positive interdependence is clearly structured; that the combination of goal and reward interdependence increases achievement over goal interdependence alone; and that resource interdependence does not increase achievement without goal interdependence.

Positive Interdependence and Intellectual Conflict

The greater the positive interdependence within a learning group, the greater the likelihood of intellectual disagreement and conflict among group members as they share their different information, perceptions, opinions, reasoning processes, theories, and conclusions (see Chapter 9). When such controversies arise, they can be constructive or destructive, depending on how they are managed and the participants' level of interpersonal and small-group skills. When managed constructively, controversy promotes uncertainty about the correctness of one's conclusions, an active search for more information, a reconceptualization of one's knowledge and conclusions, and, consequently, greater mastery and retention of the material being discussed and more frequent use of higher-level reasoning strategies (Johnson and Johnson 1979, 1989a, 1992a). Individuals working alone in competitive and individualistic situations do not have the opportunity for such intellectual challenge and, therefore, their achievement and reasoning quality suffer.

Face-to-Face Promotive Interaction

In an industrial organization it's the group effort that counts. There's really no room for stars. . . . You need talented people, but they can't do it alone. They have to have help.
              —John F. Donnelly, President, Donnelly Mirrors

Positive interdependence results in the second essential component of cooperative learning, *promotive interaction*. Promotive interaction refers to students' facilitating each other's success. While positive interdependence in and of itself may have some effect on outcomes, the face-to-face promotive interaction it fosters among individuals most powerfully influences efforts to achieve, caring and committed relationships, and psychological adjustment and social competence. Promotive interaction results in individuals:

- providing efficient and effective help and assistance to each other,
- exchanging needed resources such as information and materials,
- processing information efficiently and effectively,
- providing feedback to improve their subsequent performance,
- challenging each other's conclusions and reasoning to promote higher-quality decision making and greater insight into the problems being considered,
- encouraging each other to achieve mutual goals,
- acting in trusting and trustworthy ways,
- striving for mutual benefit, and
- supplying a moderate level of arousal with low levels of anxiety and stress.

Thus, promotive interaction enables students to encourage and facilitate each other's efforts to achieve, complete tasks, and work toward achievement of common goals.

Individual Accountability/Personal Responsibility

What children can do together today, they can do alone tomorrow.
—Vygotsky

The early settlers of Massachusetts used to say "If you do not work, you do not eat." Everyone had to do a fair share of the work. The third essential component of cooperative learning, *individual accountability*, exists when the performance of each individual student is assessed and the results are given back to the individual and to the group, who holds each person responsible for contributing a fair share to the group's success. It's important that the group knows who needs more assistance, support, and encouragement in completing a task, just as it's important that group members know they cannot "hitchhike" on the work of others. Group members sometimes seek a free ride when it's difficult to identify individuals' contributions, when their contributions are redundant, or when all members are not responsible for the final group outcome (Harkins and Petty 1982; Ingham, Levinger, Graves, and Peckham 1974;

Kerr and Bruun 1981; Latane, Williams and Harkins 1979; Moede 1927; Petty, Harkins, Williams, and Lantane 1977; Williams 1981; Williams, Harkins, and Latane 1981). This is called social loafing.

Social loafing is in direct opposition to the purpose of cooperative learning groups: to make each member a stronger individual. Individual accountability is the key to ensuring that all group members do, in fact, benefit from learning cooperatively. To ensure that each student is individually accountable for a fair share of the group's work, teachers must assess how much effort each member is contributing, provide feedback to groups and individual students, help groups avoid redundant efforts, and make sure that every member is responsible for the final outcome. After participating in a cooperative lesson, each group member should be better prepared to individually complete similar tasks.

Common ways to structure individual accountability include:

• Keeping the size of cooperative learning groups small. The smaller the size of the group, the greater the individual accountability can be.

• Giving an individual test to each student.

• Randomly examining students orally by calling on a student to present the group's work.

• Observing and recording the frequency with which each member contributes to the group's work.

• Assigning one student in each group the role of checker, who asks other group members to explain the reasoning and rationale underlying group answers.

• Having students teach what they learn to someone else, a practice called "simultaneous explaining."

There is a pattern to cooperative classroom learning—students learn together and then perform alone. They first attain knowledge and skills and learn strategies and procedures in a cooperative group. They then apply the knowledge or perform the skill, strategy, or procedure alone to demonstrate their personal mastery of the material. This pattern ensures individual accountability and allows each student to benefit as a result of working in a group.

Interpersonal and Small-Group Skills

I will pay more for the ability to deal with people than any other ability under the sun.

—John D. Rockefeller

Interpersonal and small-group skills are the fourth essential component of cooperative learning. Cooperative learning groups require students to learn academic subject matter (taskwork) and the interpersonal and small-group skills necessary to function as part of a team (teamwork). This makes cooperative learning inherently more complex than competitive or individualistic learning. If teamwork skills are not learned, taskwork cannot be completed. The greater the members' teamwork skills, the higher the quality and quantity of their learning.

In order to coordinate efforts to achieve mutual goals, students must (1) get to know and trust each other, (2) communicate accurately and unambiguously, (3) accept and support each other, and (4) resolve conflicts constructively (Johnson 1991a, 1993; Johnson and F. Johnson 1994). But students, like the rest of us, don't instinctively know how to interact effectively with others. Students must be taught the interpersonal and small-group skills required for high-quality collaboration and be motivated to use them.

The whole field of group dynamics is based on the premise that social skills are the key to group productivity (Johnson and F. Johnson 1991). The more socially skillful students are, and the more attention teachers pay to teaching and rewarding the use of social skills, the higher the achievement that can be expected within cooperative learning groups. In their studies on the long-term implementation of cooperative learning, Lew and Mesch investigated the impact of a reward contingency for using social skills along with positive interdependence and a contingency for academic achievement on performance within cooperative learning groups (Lew, Mesch, Johnson, and Johnson 1986a, 1986b; Mesch, Johnson, and Johnson 1988; Mesch, Lew, Johnson, and Johnson 1986). In the cooperative skills conditions, students were trained weekly in four social skills, with each member of a cooperative group given two bonus points toward the quiz grade if all group members were observed by the teacher demonstrating three of the four cooperative skills. The combination of positive interdependence, an academic contingency for high performance by all group members, and a social skills contingency promoted the highest achievement. One way to define a social skill for students is through a T-Chart, which we explain in Chapter 8.

Group Processing

The fifth essential component of cooperative learning is *group processing*. Effective group work is influenced by whether or not groups reflect on—process—how well they function. Group processing is defined as reflecting on a group session to (1) describe what member actions were helpful and unhelpful and (2) make decisions about what actions to continue or change. The purpose of group processing is to clarify and improve members' effectiveness in contributing to collaborative efforts to achieve the group's goals.

There are two levels of processing: small-group and whole class. In order to ensure that small-group processing takes place, teachers must allocate some time at the end of each class for cooperative groups to process how effectively members worked together. Such processing (1) enables learning groups to focus on maintaining good working relationships among members, (2) facilitates the learning of cooperative skills, (3) ensures that members receive feedback on their participation, (4) ensures that students think about their metacognitive as well as their cognitive work, and (5) provides a way to celebrate the success of the group and reinforce group members' positive behaviors. Some of the keys to successful small-group processing are:

- allowing sufficient time for it to take place,
- providing a structure for processing (such as "List three things your group is doing well today and one thing you could improve"),
- emphasizing positive feedback, making the processing specific rather than general,
- maintaining student involvement in processing,
- reminding students to use their cooperative skills during processing, and
- communicating clear expectations about the purpose of processing.

In addition to small-group processing, teachers should periodically engage in whole-class processing. When cooperative learning groups are used in a class, the teacher should observe the groups, analyze the problems they have working together, and give feedback to each group. The teacher should systematically move from group to group, possibly using a formal observation sheet, to gather specific data on each group.

At the end of the class period the teacher can conduct a whole-class processing session by sharing observation results with the class. If each group has a peer observer, results of their observations may be included to get overall class data.

Stuart Yager (Yager, Johnson, and Johnson 1985) examined the impact on achievement of (1) cooperative learning with group processing, (2) cooperative learning without group processing, and (3) individualistic learning. He found that high-, medium-, and low-achieving students in the cooperation-with-group-processing condition achieved higher on daily achievement, post-instructional achievement, and retention measures than did students in the other two conditions. Students in the cooperation-without-group-processing condition, furthermore, achieved higher on all three measures than did the students in the individualistic condition.

A follow-up study (Johnson, Johnson, Stanne, and Garibaldi 1990) compared cooperative learning with (1) no processing, (2) teacher processing (teacher-specified cooperative skills were used, then observed by the teacher who gave whole-class feedback as to how well students were using the skills), (3) teacher and student processing (as above with learning groups also discussing how well they interacted as a group), and (4) individualistic learning. Forty-nine high-ability black high school seniors and entering college freshmen at Xavier University participated in the study, which involved the students in a complex computer-assisted problem-solving assignment. The combination of teacher and student processing resulted in greater problem-solving success than did the other cooperative conditions. All three cooperative conditions resulted in higher performances than the individualistic condition.

An important aspect of both small-group and whole-class processing is group and class celebrations. Feeling successful, appreciated, and respected builds commitment to learning, enthusiasm about working in cooperative groups, and a sense of self-efficacy in terms of subject matter mastery and working cooperatively with classmates.

Using Cooperative Learning

The best answer to the question, "What is the most effective method of teaching?" is that it depends on the goal, the students, the content, and the teacher. But the next best answer is, "Students teaching other students." There is a wealth of evidence that peer teaching is extremely effective for a wide range of goals, content, and students of different levels and personalities.

—McKeachie, et al. (1986, p. 63)

Many educators who believe that they are using cooperative learning are, in fact, missing its essence. There is a crucial difference between simply putting students in groups to learn and structuring cooperation among students. Cooperation is *not* having students sit side-by-side at the same table to talk with each other as they do their individual assignments. Cooperation is *not* assigning a group report that one student does and the others put their names on. Cooperation is *not* having students do a task individually with instructions that those who finish first are to help the slower students. Cooperation is much more than being physically near other students, discussing material with other students, helping other students, or sharing material among students, although each of these is important in cooperative learning.

To be cooperative, a group must have clear positive interdependence, and members must promote each other's learning and success face-to-face, hold each other personally and individually accountable to do their fair share of the work, appropriately use interpersonal and small-group skills, and process how effectively they work together. These five essential components make small-group learning truly cooperative.

4

Formal Cooperative Learning

One of Roger's favorite demonstration science lessons is to ask students to determine how long a candle burns in a quart jar. He assigns students to groups of two, making the pairs as heterogeneous as possible. Each pair is given one candle and one quart jar (resource interdependence). He gives the instructional task of timing how long the candle will burn and the cooperative goal of deciding on one answer that both members of the pair can explain. Students are to encourage each other's participation and relate what they are learning to previous lessons (social skills). Each pair lights a candle, places the quart jar over it, and times how long the candle burns. The answers from the pairs are announced. Roger then gives the pairs the task of generating a number of answers to the question, "What factors make a difference in how long the candle burns in the jar?" The answers from the pairs are written on the board. The pairs then repeat the experiment in ways that test whether the suggested factors do in fact make a difference in how long the candle burns.

The next day students individually take a quiz on the factors affecting the time a candle burns in a quart jar (individual accountability) and their scores are totaled to determine a joint score that, if high enough, earns them bonus points (reward interdependence). They spend some time discussing the helpful actions of each member and what they could do to be even more effective in the future (group processing).

In formal cooperative learning groups students work together from one class period to several weeks to achieve shared learning goals and complete specific tasks and assignments. Formal cooperative learning groups may be used in a wide variety of ways. They can be structured for learning new information or problem solving, conducting science experiments, or working on compositions. Before exploring formal cooperative learning in depth, let's examine the teacher's role in cooperative lessons.

The Teacher's Role: Being "A Guide on the Side"

Each class session teachers must choose between being "a sage on the stage" or "a guide on the side." In doing so it's important to remember that the challenge in teaching is not *covering* the material *for* the students; it's *uncovering* the material *with* the students.

In cooperative learning situations, the teacher forms learning groups, teaches basic concepts and strategies, monitors how the learning groups function, intervenes to teach small-group skills, provides task assistance when needed, evaluates students' learning using a criterion-referenced system, and ensures that groups process how effectively members worked together. Students look to their peers for assistance, feedback, reinforcement, and support.

The teacher has a six-part role in formal cooperative learning (Johnson and Johnson 1994; Johnson, Johnson, and Holubec 1993):

1. Specifying the objectives for the lesson;

2. Making pre-instructional decisions about learning groups, room arrangement, instructional materials, and students' roles within the group;

3. Explaining the task and goal structure to the students;

4. Setting the cooperative lesson in motion;

5. Monitoring the effectiveness of the cooperative learning groups and intervening as necessary; and

6. Evaluating students' achievement and helping them discuss how well they collaborated with each other.

Specifying the Instructional Objectives

Teachers must specify two types of objectives before each lesson. The *academic objective* needs to be specified at the correct level for the students and matched to the right level of instruction according to a conceptual or task analysis. The *social skills objective* must detail the interpersonal and small-group skills that will be emphasized during the lesson. A common error many teachers make is to specify only academic objectives and ignore the social skills objectives needed to train students to cooperate effectively with each other.

Making Pre-Instructional Decisions

Deciding on the Size of the Group. Cooperative learning groups typically range in size from two to four students, but group size can vary according to the specific objectives and circumstances of a lesson. When selecting the size of a cooperative learning group, teachers must remember that the shorter the amount of time available, the smaller the group should be. Larger groups mean more resources for the group's work but also require group members to have more skills to work productively. Sometimes the materials or equipment available or the specific nature of the task may dictate a group size. The basic rule of thumb about group size is, "the smaller the better." When in doubt, it's best to go with pairs or triads.

Assigning Students to Groups. Students can be grouped in numerous ways. Perhaps the easiest and most effective way is to assign students randomly. A teacher can divide the number of students in a class by the size of the group desired and have students count off by that number (for example, 30 students divided by group size 3 equals counting off by 10). Variations of this procedure include counting off in languages other than English, or randomly handing out cards with the names of states and capitals on them and asking students to find their partners.

A related procedure is stratified random assignment where, for example, a pretest is given, the class is divided into high, medium, and low scorers, and one student from each category is randomly assigned to a triad. Or, students' learning styles can be diagnosed and one student from each category can be assigned to each learning group.

There are also teacher-selected groups. Teachers can usually put together optimal combinations of students and ensure that nonachievement-oriented students are a minority in each group or that students who trigger disruptive behavior in each other are not together.

One of our favorite methods is asking students to list three classmates with whom they would like to work. From their lists the classroom isolates (students who no one lists to work with) can be identified. The teacher can then build a group of skillful and supportive students around each isolated student.

The least recommended procedure is having students select their own groups. Student-selected groups are often homogeneous with high-achieving students, white students, minority students, males, and so on working together. Student-selected groups also tend to have less on-task behavior. A good modification is to have students list others they would like to work with and then to place each student in a learning group with one person they list and one or more teacher-selected students.

Teachers often ask three questions about assigning students to groups:

1. *Should students be placed in homogeneous or heterogeneous ability groups?* Cooperative learning groups homogeneous in ability can be used to master specific skills or to achieve certain instructional objectives. Generally, however, in heterogeneous groups students engage in more elaborative thinking, give and receive explanations more frequently, and consider a wider perspective in discussing material—all of which increase their depth of understanding, quality of reasoning, and accuracy of long-term retention.

2. Should nontask-oriented students be placed in learning groups with task-oriented peers, or be separated from them? Nonacademically-oriented students often keep on task better in a cooperative learning group with task-oriented peers.

3. How long should groups stay together? There is no formula or simple answer to this question. Some teachers keep cooperative learning groups together for an entire semester or year. Other teachers like to keep a learning group together only to complete a task, unit, or chapter. Sooner or later, however, every student should work with every other student. Our best advice is to allow groups to remain stable long enough to become successful. Breaking up groups that are having trouble functioning effectively is often counterproductive as the students don't learn the skills they need to resolve problems in collaborating with each other.

Arranging the Room. How a classroom is arranged sends a symbolic message about appropriate behavior, and the arrangement of learning groups can foster or interfere with on-task efforts. Members of a learning group should sit eye-to-eye, knee-to-knee, in other words, close enough that they can share materials, maintain eye contact with each other, talk quietly without disrupting other groups, and exchange ideas in a comfortable atmosphere. And the teacher must have a clear access lane to every group.

Choosing Instructional Materials. The choice of materials is determined by the type of task the students must complete. Once a teacher decides what is needed, the materials should be distributed among group members so that all can participate and achieve. When group members are mature and have a high level of interpersonal and small-group skills, the teacher might not have to arrange materials in any specific way. When a group is new or when members are not very skilled, however, teachers might wish to distribute materials in carefully planned ways to communicate that the assignment is to be a joint effort and that the students are in a "sink or swim together" learning situation.

Assigning Roles To Ensure Interdependence. When planning a lesson, teachers must think about the actions that will maximize student learning. They can then define those actions as "roles" and assign a role to each group member. Roles may include a summarizer, a checker of understanding, an accuracy coach, an elaborator, a researcher-runner, a recorder, an encourager of participation, and an observer (see Chapter 8 for descriptions of each role). Assigning complementary and interconnected roles to group members is effective for teaching students social skills and fostering positive interdependence.

Roles such as checking for understanding and elaborating are vital to high-quality learning but are often absent in classrooms. The role of checking for understanding, for example, focuses on periodically asking individual groupmates to explain what they are learning. From their research review, Rosenshine and Stevens (1986) concluded that "checking for comprehension" was significantly associated with higher levels of student learning and achievement. Wilson (1987) conducted a three-year, teaching-improvement study and found that the frequency of checking for understanding highly correlated with teachers' overall effectiveness. While teachers cannot continually check the understanding of every student in the class, they can engineer such checking by having students work in cooperative groups and assigning the role of checker to one member.

Explaining the Task and Goal Structure

Explaining the Academic Task. At the beginning of a lesson, the teacher must explain the academic task so that students are clear about the assignment and understand the objectives of the lesson. First, the teacher explains what the assignment is and the procedures students are to follow in completing it. Clear and specific instructions are crucial in warding off student frustration. One advantage of cooperative learning groups is that students who don't understand what they are to do can clarify the assignment and the procedures with each other before asking the teacher.

Second, the teacher explains the objectives of the lesson and relates the concepts and information to be studied to students' past experiences and learning to ensure maximum transfer and retention. The teacher can give examples to help students understand what they are to learn and do in completing the assignment. Objectives can sometimes be given as outcomes: "At the end of this lesson you will be able to explain the causes of the Civil War." Explaining the intended outcomes of the lesson increases the likelihood that students will focus on the relevant concepts and information throughout the lesson.

It's often helpful to ask class members specific questions to check their understanding of the assignment. This ensures that communication is thorough and two-way, that the assignment has been given effectively, and that the students are ready to begin. A focused discussion (see Chapter 5) may be used to help students organize in advance what they know about the content to be studied and to set students' expectations about the lesson.

Once the procedures and objectives are clear, direct teaching of concepts, principles, and strategies may take place. Relevant concepts can be defined and teachers can answer any questions students have about the concepts or facts they are to learn or apply during the lesson.

Explaining Criteria for Success and Desired Behaviors. Students need to know what level of performance is expected of them. Academic expectations are expressed as preset criteria that establish what is and is not acceptable work (rather than grading students on a curve). In other words, evaluation within cooperatively structured lessons needs to be criterion-referenced. A teacher may say, "Everyone who earns 95 points or more will get an A, scores between 90 and 94 points will be given a B, and scores between 85 and 89 points will be given a C. The group is not finished until all members score above 85." Or a teacher may say, "The group is not finished until every member has demonstrated mastery." Sometimes, improvement (doing better this week than last week) can be set as the criterion of excellence. To promote intergroup cooperation, teachers may also set criteria for the whole class to reach.

Because the word "cooperation" has many different connotations and uses, in addition to explaining criteria for success, teachers need to specify the behaviors that are appropriate and desirable within learning groups. Beginning (forming) behaviors include "stay with your group and do not wander around the room," "use quiet voices," "take turns," and "use each other's names." When groups begin to function effectively, they can be expected to:

- Have each member explain how to get the answer.
- Ask each member to relate what is being learned to previous learnings.
- Check to make sure everyone in the group understands the material and agrees with the answers.
- Encourage everyone to participate.
- Listen accurately to what other group members are saying.
- Not change their minds unless they are logically persuaded (majority rule does not promote learning).
- Critique ideas, not people.

It's important for teachers to be specific when discussing desirable behavior with students. Teachers should operationally define each social skill using a "T-Chart" (see Chapter 8, Figure 8.1). Emphasizing one or two behaviors at a time is enough. Students need to know what behavior is appropriate and desirable within a cooperative learning group, but they should not be subjected to information overload.

It's also important for students to practice skills more than once or twice. Teachers must continue to emphasize a skill until students have integrated it into their behavioral repertoires and do it automatically and habitually.

Setting the Cooperative Lesson in Motion

During formal cooperative lessons, students' actions can be loosely or highly prescribed. Students can improvise procedures as they go along, or they can follow explicit scripts (Johnson and Johnson 1994). Different teachers like to provide different degrees of structure. And there is a wide range of possibilities.

At one end of the continuum, cooperative learning can be given minimal structure. Cooperative lessons can be structured to specify only positive goal interdependence and individual accountability, emphasize a few social skills, and provide some group processing at the end. Additional structure can be added by specifying complementary roles for students to engage in as they work together or arranging materials so that students must depend on each other's resources to complete the assignment.

At the other end of the continuum are highly structured direct approaches to cooperative learning that must be used in a prescribed, lockstep manner. These include cooperative scripts, structures, and curriculum packages that specify, step-by-step, what each student is to do throughout the lesson.

Cooperative learning scripts are standard, content-free cooperative procedures for either conducting generic, repetitive lessons (such as writing reports or giving presentations) or managing classroom routines (such as checking homework and reviewing tests). Donald Dansereau and his colleagues (1985) have developed a number of cooperative scripts that structure student interaction. One of their best known is a simple text-processing script called MURDER (Mobilize, Understand, Recall, Detect, Elaborate, Review). In this script, students are assigned to pairs and first *mobilize* their resources for learning by (1) establishing an appropriate mood and (2) surveying the text to establish cooperative action points (asterisks in the margin to indicate where they will stop reading and engage in cooperative information processing). Both partners then silently read for *understanding* until they reach the first action point. One partner *recalls/recites* what has been learned to that point while the other partner *detects* and corrects errors and omissions. Both partners then collaboratively *elaborate* on the material by forming images, analogies, and direct connections to other information. They then continue reading silently for understanding until they reach the next action point where they reverse roles and repeat the recall, detect, and elaboration steps. The partners proceed through the material, alternating roles until they have completed the assignment. They then cooperatively *review* and organize the entire body of information, once again alternating active and monitoring roles.

Spencer Kagan (1988) has identified a number of cooperative learning structures. A simple structure is a three-step interview, in which students are assigned to pairs, student A interviews student B, student B interviews student A, and the two share the results with another pair. Co-op Co-op (Kagan 1988) assigns students to heterogeneous cooperative learning groups, assigns each group one part of a learning unit, and provides each group member a mini-topic to complete alone and then present to the group. Each group then synthesizes the mini-topics of its members into a group presentation for the whole class.

Similar to Co-Op Co-Op, Group Investigation (Sharan and Hertz-Lazarowitz 1980) is a complex structure in which students form cooperative groups according to common interests in a topic. All group members help plan how to research their topic. They then divide the work among themselves, and each group member carries out a part of the investigation. The group synthesizes and summarizes its work and presents the findings to the class.

In Jigsaw (Aronson 1978), students are assigned to cooperative groups, all groups are assigned the same topic, and each member is given one unique section of the topic to learn and then teach to the other members of the group. Members study the topic individually and then make a presentation to the group. The group synthesizes the presentations of the members into the whole picture. In studying the life of Sojourner Truth, for example, each group member is given material on a part of her life, but no student can learn about her whole life unless all members teach their parts.

A *cooperative curriculum package* is a set of curriculum materials specifically designed to contain cooperative learning as well as academic content. Teams-Games-Tournament (TGT) is a combination of group cooperation, intergroup competition, and instructional games (DeVries and Edwards 1974). It begins with the teacher directly teaching a lesson. Students then meet in cooperative learning teams of four or five members (a mixture of high, medium, and low achievers) to complete a set of worksheets on the lesson. They then participate in games as representatives of their teams. Who competes with whom is modified each week to ensure that students compete with classmates who achieve at a similar level. The highest scoring teams are publicly recognized in a weekly class newsletter. Grades are given on the basis of individual performance.

TGT's development was followed by the development of a number of other curriculum packages by one of David DeVries' doctoral students, Robert Slavin. Student-Team-Achievement-Divisions Learning (STAD) (Slavin 1980) is a modification of TGT that substitutes a weekly quiz for playing an academic game. Teams receive recognition for the sum of the improvement scores of team members.

Team-Assisted-Individualization (TAI) is a highly individualized math curriculum for grades 3 to 6 in which students work individually to complete math assignments using self-instructional (programmed learning) curriculum materials (Slavin 1985). Students are assigned to four- or five-member teams, but team members do not work together. Instead, they check each other's answers, administer tests, and provide help when another member requests it. Because the curriculum units are designed to be self-explanatory and team members are usually working at quite different levels, cooperative interaction is held to a minimum. Team scores are computed weekly and team members are given certificates on the basis of how much work each member completes. Students are graded strictly on their own work.

Cooperative Integrated Reading and Composition (CIRC) is a set of curriculum materials that supplement basal readers and ensure that cooperative learning is applied to reading, writing, spelling, and language mechanics (Stevens, Madden, Slavin, and Farnish 1987). CIRC divides the class into two reading groups of 8 to 15 members; one group focuses on phonic decoding and comprehension skills (code/meaning) and the other focuses on comprehension and inference skills (meaning). Students are assigned to a pair within the reading group and then combined with a pair from the other reading group. Assignments are given to the groups of four to complete either as pairs or as a whole group. Students' scores on all quizzes, compositions, and book reports contribute to a team score and certificates are awarded. Students are graded on their own work.

No matter which cooperative procedure is used, the teacher has to monitor the students at work and intervene when necessary.

Monitoring the Effectiveness of Cooperative Learning Groups and Intervening as Necessary

Whether the lesson is loosely or tightly structured cooperatively, the teacher's role is to monitor students' interaction in the learning groups and intervene to help students learn and interact more skillfully.

Monitoring Student Behavior and Providing Task Assistance. The teacher's job begins in earnest when the cooperative learning groups start working. Teachers observe the interaction among group members to assess their academic progress and appropriate use of interpersonal and small-group skills. Observations can be formal with an observation schedule on which frequencies are tallied, or anecdotal, with informal descriptions of students' statements and actions.

By carefully listening to students explain what they are learning to each other, teachers can determine what students do and do not understand. Through cooperative work students make hidden thinking processes overt and subject to observation and commentary and teachers are able to observe how students are constructing their understanding of the assigned material and intervene when necessary to increase understanding. A variety of observation instruments and procedures can be found in Johnson and F. Johnson (1991) and in Johnson, Johnson, and Holubec (1993).

In monitoring the groups as they work, teachers need to clarify instructions, review important procedures and strategies for completing the assignment, answer questions, and teach task skills as necessary. In discussing the concepts and information to be learned, teachers need to use the language or terms relevant to the learning. Instead of saying, *"Yes, that's right,"* teachers should say something more specific to the assignment, such as, *"Yes, that is one way to find the main idea of a paragraph."* The use of the more specific statement reinforces the desired learning and promotes positive transfer by helping the students associate a term with their learning.

One way to intervene is to interview a cooperative learning group by asking them "What are you doing?" "Why are you doing it?" and "How will it help you?"

Intervening To Teach Social Skills. While monitoring learning groups, teachers may find students without the necessary social skills to be effective group members. In these cases the teacher needs to intervene and suggest to the group more effective procedures for working together and specific social skills to use. Teachers may also intervene to reinforce particularly effective and skillful behaviors they notice.

Teachers should not intervene in the groups any more than is absolutely necessary. Most teachers are geared to jumping in and solving problems for students to get them back on track. With a little patience, however, teachers find that cooperative groups can often work their way through their own problems (task and maintenance) and acquire not only a solution, but also a method of solving similar problems in the future. Choosing when to intervene and when not to is part of the art of teaching. Even when intervening, teachers can turn the problem back to the group to solve. Many teachers intervene in a group by having members set aside their task, pointing out the problem, and asking the group to create three possible solutions and decide which solution to try first. The social skills required for productive group work, along with activities that may be used to teach them, are described in Johnson and F. Johnson (1991) and Johnson (1991, 1993).

Evaluating Learning and Processing Interaction

Providing Closure to the Lesson. Informal cooperative learning procedures are often used to provide closure to lessons by having students summarize the major points in the lesson, recall ideas, and identify final questions for the teacher (see Chapter 5). At the end of the lesson students should be able to summarize what they have learned and understand how they will use it in future lessons.

Evaluating the Quality and Quantity of Students' Learning. Tests should be given and papers and presentations should be graded. Group members' learning must be evaluated by a criterion-referenced system for cooperative learning to be successful. Furthermore, cooperative learning provides an arena in which performance-based assessment (requiring students to demonstrate what they can do with what they know by performing a procedure or skill), authentic assessment (requiring students to demonstrate the desired procedure or skill in a real-life context), and total quality learning (continuous improvement of the process of students helping teammates learn) can take place. A wide variety of assessment formats can be used and students can be directly involved in assessing each other's level of learning and providing immediate remediation to ensure all group members' learning is maximized.

Processing How Well the Group Functioned. When students have completed an assignment, or run out of time, they should be asked to engage in small-group or whole-class processing (see Chapter 3). When structuring small-group processing, teachers should avoid questions that can be answered with "yes" or "no." Instead of saying, "Did everyone help each other learn?" the teacher should say, "How frequently did each member explain how to solve a problem and correct or clarify another member's explanation?" Feedback should be descriptive and specific, not evaluative and general (see Johnson 1993).

A common teaching error is to provide too brief a time for students to process the quality of their cooperation. Students don't learn from experiences they don't reflect on. If the learning groups are to function better tomorrow than they did today, students must receive feedback, reflect on how their actions may be more effective, and plan how to be even more skillful during the next group session.

Any assignment in any subject area may be structured cooperatively. The teacher decides on the objectives of the lesson, makes a number of pre-instructional decisions about the size of the group and the materials required to conduct the lesson, explains to students the task and the cooperative goal structure, monitors the groups as they work, intervenes when it is necessary, and then evaluates student learning and ensures that groups process how effectively they are functioning.

One of the things we have been told many times by teachers who have mastered the use of cooperative learning is, "Don't say it's easy!" We know it's not. It can take years to become an expert. There's a lot of pressure to teach like everyone else, to have students learn alone, and not to let students look at each other's papers. Students will not be accustomed to working together and are likely to have a competitive orientation. Teachers may wish to start small by taking one topic or one class, using cooperative learning until they feel comfortable and then expanding its use into other topics or classes. In essence, teachers learn an *expert system* (a conceptual understanding of the five essential components and the teacher's role) of how to implement cooperative learning, which they use to create lessons uniquely tailored to their students, curriculum, needs, and teaching circumstances. The use of cooperative learning is based on a conceptual, metacognitive under-standing of its nature. *Implementing cooperative learning is not easy, but it's worth the effort.*

5

Informal Cooperative Learning

At times, teachers need to lecture, show a movie or videotape, give a demonstration, or have a guest speaker. In such cases, informal cooperative learning can be used to ensure that students are cognitively active. Informal cooperative learning consists of having students work together to achieve a joint learning goal in temporary, ad-hoc groups that last from a few minutes to one class period. These groups can be used to focus student attention on the material to be learned, set a mood conducive to learning, help organize in advance the material to be covered in a class session, ensure that students cognitively process the material being taught, and provide closure to an instructional session. *Informal cooperative learning groups* also ensure that misconceptions, incorrect understandings, and gaps in understanding are identified and corrected, and that learning experiences are personalized. They can be used at any time, but are especially useful during a lecture or direct teaching.

During lecturing and direct teaching, the teacher's instructional challenge is to ensure that students do the intellectual work of organizing, explaining, summarizing, and integrating new material into existing conceptual networks. This can be achieved by having students do advance organizing, cognitively process what they are learning, and provide closure to the lesson. Breaking up lectures with short periods of cooperative processing leaves slightly less lecture time, but helps counter what is proclaimed as the main problem of lectures: *The information passes from the notes of the professor to the notes of the student without passing through the mind of either one.*

FIGURE 5.1

Informal Cooperative Learning

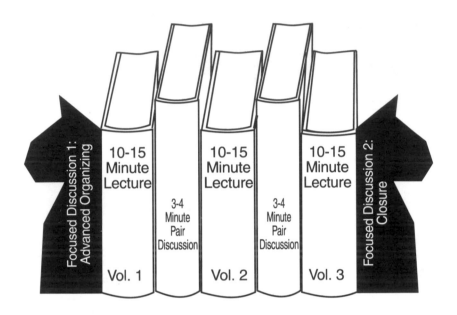

The following procedure helps teachers plan a lecture that keeps students actively engaged intellectually. It entails having focused discussions before and after the lecture (i.e., bookends) and interspersing pair discussions throughout the lecture.

1. *Focused Discussion 1: Advanced Organizing.* Assign students to pairs. The person nearest them will do. Requiring different seating arrangements each class period allows students to meet and interact with a number of other students in the class. Give the pairs the cooperative assignment of completing the initial (advance organizer) task. Give them only four or five minutes to do so. The discussion task is aimed at promoting advance organizing of what the students know about the topic to be presented and establishing expectations about what the lecture will cover.

2. *Lecture Segment 1.* Deliver the first segment of the lecture. This segment should be 10 to 15 minutes long—that's about the length of time

a motivated adult can concentrate on a lecture; for unmotivated adolescents, the time may be shorter.

3. *Pair Discussion 1*. Give the pairs of students a three- to four-minute discussion task focused on the material just presented. This ensures that students are actively thinking about the material being presented. The discussion task may be (a) to give an answer to a question posed by the teacher, (b) to give a reaction to the theory, concepts, or information being presented, or (c) to relate material to past learning so that it gets integrated into existing conceptual frameworks (i.e., elaborate the material being presented). Discussion pairs respond to the task in the following way:

a. Each student *formulates* an answer.

b. Students *share* their answers with their partners.

c. Students *listen* carefully to their partners' answers.

d. Pairs *create* a new answer that is superior to each member's initial formulation through the process of association, building on each other's thoughts, and synthesizing.

It's important that students are randomly called on to share their answers after each discussion task. Randomly choose two or three students to give 30-second summaries of their discussions. Such individual accountability ensures that the pairs take tasks seriously and check to ensure that both students in each pair are prepared to answer.

4. *Lecture Segment 2*. Deliver the second segment of the lecture.

5. *Pair Discussion 2*. Give a discussion task similar to the previous one focused on the second part of the lecture.

6. Repeat this sequence of lecture segment and pair discussion until the lecture is complete.

7. *Focused Discussion 2: Closure*. It's necessary to give an ending discussion task to summarize what students have learned from the lecture. Pairs of students should have four or five minutes to summarize and discuss the material covered in the lecture. The discussion should result in students integrating what they have just learned into existing conceptual frameworks. The task may also point students toward what the homework will cover or what will be presented in the next class session. This provides closure to the lecture.

8. Process the procedure with students regularly to help them increase their skill and speed in completing short discussion tasks. Processing questions may include: "How well prepared were you to complete

the discussion tasks?" and "How could you come even better prepared tomorrow?"

The informal cooperative learning group is not only effective for getting students actively involved in understanding what they are learning during a lecture, it also provides time for teachers to gather their wits, reorganize notes, take a deep breath, and move around the class listening to what students are saying. Listening to student discussions can give teachers direction and insight into how well concepts are being grasped by students (who probably don't have graduate degrees in the topic being presented, after all).

Besides the use of formal and informal cooperative learning groups, there is a need for permanent cooperative base groups that provide relatively long-term relationships among students. It's to this use of cooperative learning that we now turn.

6

Cooperative Base Groups

Cooperative base groups are long-term cooperative learning groups with stable membership whose primary responsibilities are to help students provide each other with support, encouragement, and assistance in completing assignments and hold each other accountable for striving to learn. Typically, cooperative base groups (1) are heterogeneous in membership (especially in terms of achievement, motivation, and task orientation), (2) meet regularly (daily or biweekly), and (3) last for at least the duration of a class (a semester or year) and preferably until the students are graduated. When students know that the cooperative base group will stay together until each member is graduated, they become committed to finding ways to motivate and encourage their groupmates. Problems in working with each other cannot be ignored or waited out.

The activities for base groups can include:

• *Academic support tasks* such as checking to see what assignments each member has and what assistance is needed. Members can give each other advice on how to study and "survive" in school. They can prepare each other to take tests and go over the questions missed after the test. And they can share their areas of expertise (such as art or computers) with each other. Above all, members monitor each other's academic progress and make sure all members are achieving.

• *Routine tasks* such as taking attendance or collecting homework.

• *Personal support tasks* such as listening sympathetically when a member has problems with parents or friends, having general discussions about life, giving each other advice about relationships, and helping each other solve nonacademic problems. Teachers may increase the likelihood of personal support through trust-building exercises, such as having members share their favorite movie, a childhood experience, a memory, and so forth.

Base groups can be used two ways. The first is to have a base group in each course. Class base groups stay together only for the duration of the course. The second is to organize all students within the school into base groups and have the groups function as an essential part of school life for at least a year and preferably until all members are graduated.

Class Base Groups

The larger the class and the more complex the subject matter, the more important it is to have class base groups. Base group members should exchange phone numbers and information about schedules so they can meet outside of class if they wish. At the beginning of each session, class members meet in their base groups to:

1. Greet each other and check to see that none of their group is under undue stress. The two questions to discuss are: "How are you today?" and "Are we all prepared for this class period?"

2. Check to see if members have completed their homework or need help and assistance in doing so. The questions to be answered are: "Did you do your homework?" and "Is there anything you did not understand?" If group members don't have time to help each other during the base group meeting, they can make appointments to meet during free time or lunch. Periodically, the base groups may be given a checklist of academic skills and asked to assess which ones each member needs to practice.

3. Review what members have read and done since the last class session. Members should be able to give a brief summary of what they have read, thought about, and done. They may come to class with resources they have found and want to share, or copies of work they have completed and wish to distribute to their base group members.

4. Get to know each other better and provide positive feedback by discussing such questions as: "What do you like about yourself?" and "What is the best thing that has happened to you this week?"

Class base groups support individual group members. If a group member arrives late, or must leave early one day, the group can provide information about what the student missed. Additionally, group members can assist one another with assignments such as writing required papers. In base groups, assignments can be discussed; papers can be planned, reviewed, and edited; and any questions regarding assignments and class sessions can be first addressed. If a group is unable to resolve an issue, it can then be brought to the teachers' attention.

Some attention should be paid to building a base group identity and group cohesion. The first week the base groups meet, for example, each can pick a name, design a flag, or choose a motto. If a teacher with the proper expertise is available, the groups will benefit from participating in a "challenge course" involving ropes and obstacles. Having groups undertake this type of physical challenge together builds cohesion quickly.

All members are expected to contribute actively to class discussions, work to maintain effective working relationships with other participants, complete all assignments, assist classmates in completing their assignments, express their ideas, change their minds only when persuaded by logic or new information, and indicate agreement with base group's work by signing a weekly contract.

School Base Groups

At the beginning of the academic year, students should be assigned to school base groups (or the base groups from the previous year should be reconvened). Class schedules should be arranged so that members of base groups are assigned to as many of the same classes as possible. School base groups should stay together for at least a year; ideally, until all members are graduated. During the year, school base groups meet twice a day to twice a week.

When base groups meet twice each day, they meet first thing in the morning and last thing in the afternoon. At the beginning of each day students meet to welcome each other to school, check to see if everyone has completed and understands their homework, and just get to know and connect with each other better.

At the end of the day members meet in their base groups to see that everyone is taking their homework home, understands the assignments to be completed, and has the help and assistance they need to do their work. In addition, base groups might wish to discuss what members have learned during the day and check to see what plans members have for the evening. During the evening students can confer on the telephone or even study together.

When base groups meet twice each week (perhaps first thing on Monday and last thing on Friday), they meet to discuss each member's academic progress, provide help and assistance to each other, hold each member accountable for completing assignments and progressing satisfactorily through the academic program, and just get to know each other. The Monday morning meeting refocuses students on school, provides any emotional support required after the weekend, reestablishes personal contact among base group members, and helps students set their academic goals for the week (i.e., decide what is still to be done on assignments that are due and so forth). Members should carefully review each other's assignments and ensure that everyone has the help and assistance needed for the week.

The Friday afternoon meeting lets students review the week, set academic goals for the weekend (e.g., what homework has to be done before Monday), and share weekend plans.

The Advisee or Homeroom Base Group

In many schools it will seem difficult to implement base groups. Two opportunities are advisor/advisee groups and homerooms. Teachers may divide their advisee group into base groups and then plan an agenda for them to follow during a daily or weekly meeting. Or homeroom time can be spent having students meet in base groups.

In one school we work with, each teacher is assigned a group of advisees to meet with once a week. The meeting lasts for 30 minutes. Teachers divide their advisees into base groups, which are given four tasks:

1. A quick *self-disclosure task* such as answering the questions: "What is the most exciting thing you did over break?" "What is the worst thing that happened to you last weekend?" "What is your biggest fear?" "What is your favorite ice cream flavor?"

2. An *administrative task* such as choosing what classes to register for next semester.

3. An *academic task* such as writing out three pieces of advice for taking tests. The advice can be typed up and distributed the following week.

4. A *closing task* such as wishing each other good luck for the day or week.

Need for Long-Term, Stable Relationships

Cooperative base groups help students establish long-term, permanent relationships, which are important for several reasons. First, most relationships in schools are, at best, shipboard romances. Relationships are temporary because in most schools it is assumed that classmates and teachers are replaceable parts in the education machine and, therefore, any classmate or teacher will do in any situation. It's important that some of the relationships built in schools be permanent. The longer a cooperative group exists, the more influence members will have on each other, the more caring their relationships will become, the greater the social support they will provide for each other, and the more committed they will be to each other's success. Permanent cooperative base groups provide the arena in which caring and committed relationships can be created that improve attendance, personalize the school experience, increase achievement, and improve the quality of life within the classroom and school.

Second, long-term relationships promote concern for others as well as oneself and provide an opportunity to express that concern. A balance between concern for self and concern for others is increasingly important. Many high school and college students' own pleasures and pains, successes and failures occupy center stage in their lives (Conger 1988, Seligman 1988). Each person tends to focus on achieving personal ends without concern for others. Physical, psychological, and material self-indulgence have become a primary concern (Conger 1988, NASSP 1984).

Over the past 20 years, self-interest has become more important than commitment to society. Young adults have turned away from careers of public service to careers of self-service. Many young adults have a delusion of individualism, believing that they are separate and apart from all other individuals and, therefore, others' frustration, unhappiness, hunger, despair, and misery have no significant bearing on their own well-being. This is false. With the increase over the past two decades in adolescents' and youths' concern for personal well-being, there has been a corresponding decrease in concern for the welfare of others (particularly the less advantaged) and for society itself (Astin, Green, Korn, and Schalit 1986). Self-orientation interferes with consideration of others' needs as it actively prevents concern for others as equally deserving persons.

Third, long-term relationships can motivate students to work hard and do their best by holding them accountable for doing so. Numerous students spend very little time studying, avoid hard subjects, and simply coast along, doing far less than they are capable of doing. Long-term, persistent efforts to achieve come from the heart, not from the head. And the heart is reached through relationships, not intellectual appeals.

Fourth, long-term relationships can change students' attitudes. Students need to value education, aspire to post-secondary education, and want to learn. Such attitudes are changed primarily through personal relationships (not information), in groups, as the result of discussions that lead to public commitment to study hard and take education more seriously, and as the result of personal appeals made by friends whose opinions are valued (Johnson and F. Johnson 1991).

Finally, long-term relationships provide a means of both preventing and combating the school dropout rate. Any student who believes that "in this school, no one knows me, no one cares about me, no one would miss me if I were gone," is at risk of dropping out. Base groups provide a set of personal and supportive relationships that may keep many students from feeling this way. Dropping out often results from being alienated from the school and the other students. Base groups can subtly and overtly fight a student's inclination to drop out. If a student does become at risk, a teacher can approach his base group and say, "Roger's thinking about dropping out of school. Go find him and talk to him. We're not going to lose Roger without a fight."

Cooperative base groups can be used at any level to provide students with a support network. When used in conjunction with formal and informal cooperative learning, base groups help students reinforce lessons learned in class, double-check their understand of lesson content and assignments, and establish meaningful relationships with peers. Cooperative base groups help students help each other and themselves, thus helping to create a cooperative school culture.

7

Integrated Use of Cooperative Learning in the Classroom

As we've said, any lesson at any grade level can be structured cooperatively. All classes can have a mixture of cooperative formal, informal, and base groups and can use cooperative learning scripts to different degrees. A typical class session consists of a base group meeting, a short lecture or a group project, and an ending base group meeting. The instructor formally starts the class by welcoming the students and instructing them to meet in their base groups for the introduction and warm-up task. The teacher then has three choices. She can (1) give a lecture using informal cooperative learning groups, (2) have students complete an assignment in formal cooperative learning groups, or (3) present a short lecture and assign a short group assignment. At the end of the class session students meet in their base groups to summarize and synthesize what they have learned. This structure keeps students intellectually and emotionally tuned in to the work at hand and school in general.

An example of the integrated use of the types of cooperative learning is as follows. Students arriving in class in the morning gather in base groups to do a self-disclosure task (such as answering the question, "what is each member's favorite television show?"), check each other's homework to make sure all members understand the academic material and are prepared for the day, and tell each other to have a great day.

Their teacher, Ms. Bajek, then begins a lesson on world interdependence. The objectives for the lesson are for students to learn about global economic interdependence and to improve their skill in encouraging each other's participation. Ms. Bajek has a series of objects and wants students to identify all the countries involved in creating the objects. To help students cognitively organize in advance what they know about the world economy, Ms. Bajek uses informal cooperative learning by asking students to turn to the person seated next to them and identify the seven continents and one product produced in each continent. They have four minutes to do so.

Formal cooperative learning is then used in the lesson. Ms. Bajek has her 30 students count off from 1 to 10 to form random triads. Students sit so they can either face each other or her. Ms. Bajek hands out the objects, which include a silk shirt with plastic buttons, a cup of tea (a saucer and cup with a tea bag and a lump of sugar in it), and a hand-held cassette player with earphones (with a cassette tape of a Nashville star) made by Phillips (a European company). She assigns members of each triad the roles of hypothesizer (who hypothesizes about the number of products in each item and where they came from), reference guide (who looks up each hypothesized country in the book to see what products it exports), and recorder (for more about roles, see Chapter 8). After the preliminary tasks are completed for each item the roles are rotated so that each student fulfills each role once.

Ms. Bajek introduces world economic interdependence by noting that:

1. Global economic interdependence is almost beyond imagining.

2. A hand-held calculator most often contains electronic chips from the United States; is assembled in Singapore or Indonesia; is placed in a steel housing from India; and is stamped with a label "Made in Japan" on arrival in Yokohama (the trees and chemicals used for the label's paper and ink are all grown and processed elsewhere as are the plastic in the calculator's keys and body).

3. Modern hotels in Saudi Arabia are built with room modules made in Brazil, construction labor from South Korea, and management from the United States.

Ms. Bajek then assigns the academic task of identifying how many countries contributed to the production of each object. She establishes positive goal interdependence by stating that it is a cooperative assignment and, therefore, all members of the group must agree on an answer before it is recorded and all members must be able to explain each of the group's answers. The criteria for success are to hand in a correctly completed report form and for each member to score 90 percent or better on the test to be given the next day on world economic interdependence. Ms. Bajek establishes positive reward interdependence by stating that if the record sheet is accurate, each member will receive 15 points and if all members of the group achieve 90 percent or better on the test, each member will receive 5 bonus points. Individual accountability is established by the roles assigned and the individual test. In addition, Ms. Bajek will observe each group to make sure all students are participating and learning. She informs students that the expected social skill to be used by all students is encouraging each other's participation. She defines the skill and has each student practice it twice before the lesson begins.

While students work in their groups, Ms. Bajek monitors their progress by systematically observing each group and intervening to provide academic assistance and help in using the interpersonal and small-group skills required to work together effectively. At the end of the lesson the groups hand in their report forms to be evaluated and process how well they worked together by identifying three things members did to help the group and one thing that could be added to improve their group next time.

Next, Ms. Bajek uses a generic cooperative lesson script to teach vocabulary. Studying vocabulary words is a routine that occurs every week in this class. She instructs students to move into their vocabulary pairs and, for each vocabulary word identified in the world interdependence lesson, to (a) write down what they think the word means, (b) look it up in the text and write down its official definition, (c) write a sentence in which the word is used, and (d) learn how to spell the word. When the students have done that for each word, the pair is to make up a story in which all of the words are used. Pairs then exchange stories and carefully determine whether all the words are used appropriately and spelled correctly. If not, the two pairs discuss the word until everyone is clear about what it means and how it should be used.

Ms. Bajek uses informal cooperative learning to provide closure to the lesson by asking students to meet with a person from another group and write out four conclusions they derived from the lesson and circle the one they believe is most important.

At the end of the school day the cooperative base groups meet to review what students believe is the most important thing they have learned during the day, the homework that has been assigned, and the help each member needs to complete the homework, and to tell each other to have a fun afternoon and evening.

The combination of formal and informal cooperative learning and cooperative base groups along with cooperative structures is an effective way to structure any lesson or class at any level. It is up to classroom teachers to decide which forms of cooperative learning to use for which learning tasks. Teachers may take years to develop the expertise necessary to structure cooperation automatically into lessons. Once teachers reach this level and students learn cooperative skills, schools become places where worthy goals are reached. It is to the teaching of cooperative skills that we now turn.

8

Teaching Students Cooperative Skills

Instead of looking on discussion as a stumbling block in the way of action, we think it an indispensable preliminary to any wise action at all.

—Pericles

The Importance of Cooperative Skills

Children are not born knowing instinctively how to interact effectively with others, and interpersonal and group skills do not magically appear when they are needed. Many elementary and secondary students lack basic social skills such as the ability to correctly identify others' emotions or appropriately discuss an assignment. Thus, many teachers structuring lessons cooperatively initially find their students unable to collaborate with each other. But it is within cooperative situations, where there is a task to complete, that social skills become most relevant and should ideally be taught. All students need to become skillful in communicating, building and maintaining trust, providing leadership, engaging in fruitful controversy, and managing conflict (Johnson 1991, 1993; Johnson and F. Johnson 1991). Therefore, teaching cooperative skills becomes an important prerequisite for academic learning because achievement improves as students become more effective in learning from each other.

Teaching Cooperative Skills: General Rules

Four general rules undergird the teaching of cooperative skills. *The first is that a cooperative context must be established prior to teaching cooperative skills.* Cooperative learning is intended to create a perception that students "sink or swim together" and, therefore, must be actively involved in maximizing their own learning as well as the learning of groupmates. When this overall cooperative goal is lacking, interaction among students becomes competitive, hostile, divisive, and destructive. Students who are competing want to "win," not learn the skills to cooperate. Similarly, students who spend all day working alone see no reason to learn to cooperate and have no chance to learn cooperative skills. Therefore, implementing cooperative learning is vital to increasing students' collaborative competencies.

Second, cooperative skills must be directly taught. Structuring lessons cooperatively is not enough. Learning how to interact effectively with others is no different from learning how to use a microscope, play a piano, write a complete sentence, or read. Instruction in cooperative skills, like all skill instruction, must be done directly and reinforced.

Third, while the teacher structures cooperation within the classroom and initially defines the skills required to collaborate, the other group members largely determine whether or not the skills are learned and internalized. Teachers rely on class members to cue and monitor each other's use of cooperative skills, give feedback on how well the skills are being enacted, and reinforce their appropriate use. Peer accountability to learn cooperative skills must always be coupled with peer support for doing so. Group members must communicate that they want each other to practice the collaborative skills and that they are there to help each other do so. After the teacher instructs students as to what the cooperative skills are, and encourages students to practice the skills in their learning groups, peer support and feedback determine whether the skills are used appropriately and frequently enough to become natural and automatic actions. Peer feedback occurs subtly while the groups are working and directly in formal feedback sessions.

Fourth, the earlier students are taught cooperative skills, the better. There are procedures for kindergarten and even preschool teachers to use in teaching students collaborative skills. Elementary, secondary, and post-secondary teachers should be very involved in improving students' collaboration competencies. Informing adults who are already engineers, managers, supervisors, or secretaries that they need to learn how to cooperate more effectively with others is important, but probably a little late. A direct relation exists between schools demanding that students work individually and the number of adults in our society who lack the competencies required to work effectively with others in career, family, and leisure settings. Their education should have prepared them for the cooperation inherent in adult career and family life.

What Skills Need To Be Taught?

Numerous interpersonal skills affect the success of collaborative efforts (Johnson 1991, 1993; Johnson and F. Johnson 1991; Johnson and R. Johnson 1994). Which cooperative skills teachers emphasize in their classes depends on what their students have mastered. As teachers observe and monitor their students working in cooperative learning groups they notice where students lack important skills. There are four levels of cooperative skills:

1. *Forming*—the bottom-line skills needed to establish a functioning cooperative learning group.

2. *Functioning*—the skills needed to manage the group's activities in completing the task and maintain effective working relationships among members.

3. *Formulating*—the skills needed to build deeper-level understanding of the material being studied, to stimulate the use of higher-quality reasoning strategies, and to maximize mastery and retention of the assigned material.

4. *Fermenting*—the skills needed to stimulate reconceptualization of the material being studied, cognitive conflict, the search for more information, and communication of the rationale behind one's conclusions.

The following list of required student behaviors is a starting point for examining students' skillfulness relative to the four levels of cooperative skills.

Forming

Forming skills are an initial set of management skills directed toward organizing learning groups and establishing minimum norms for appropriate behavior. Here are some of the more important behaviors related to forming skills:

• Moving into cooperative learning groups without undue noise or bothering others. Work time in groups is a valuable commodity so as little time as necessary should be spent rearranging furniture and moving into learning groups. Students may need to practice the procedure for getting into groups several times before they become efficient in doing so.

• Staying with the group. Students who move around the room during group time are nonproductive and distract other group members.

• Using quiet voices. Although learning groups rely on personal interaction, they don't need to be overly noisy. Some teachers assign one student in each group to make sure that everyone speaks softly.

• Encouraging everyone to participate. All group members need to share their ideas and materials and be part of the group's efforts to achieve. Having students take turns is one way to formalize whole-group participation.

• Keeping hands (and feet) away from others.

• Looking at the materials being studied.

• Calling group members by name.

• Looking at the speaker.

• Eliminating "put-downs."

Functioning

Functioning skills, the second level of cooperative skills, are directed at managing the group's efforts to complete tasks and maintain effective working relationships. The mixture of keeping members on task, finding effective and efficient work procedures, and fostering a pleasant and friendly work atmosphere is vital for effective leadership in cooperative learning groups. Functioning skills include:

• Giving direction to the group's work by (1) stating and restating the purpose of the assignment, (2) setting or calling attention to time limits, and (3) offering procedures on how to most effectively complete an assignment.

• Expressing support and acceptance, both verbally and nonverbally, through eye contact, interest, praise, and seeking others' ideas and conclusions.

• Asking for help or clarification of what is being said or done in the group.

• Offering to explain or clarify.

• Paraphrasing another member's contributions.

• Energizing the group when motivation is low by suggesting new ideas, using humor, or being enthusiastic.

• Describing one's feelings when appropriate.

Formulating

Formulating skills, the third level of cooperative skills, provide the mental processes needed to build deeper understanding of the material being studied, to stimulate the use of higher-quality reasoning strategies, and to maximize mastery and retention of the assigned material. Because the purpose of learning groups is to maximize the learning of all members, these are skills specifically aimed at providing formal methods for processing the material being studied. Formulating skills can be carried out as group members fill different roles. Roles associated with these skills include:

• Summarizer, who summarizes out loud what has just been read or discussed as completely as possible without referring to notes or to the original material. All the important ideas and facts should be included in the summary. Every member of the group must summarize from memory often to maximize their learning.

• Corrector, who seeks accuracy by correcting a member's summary and adding important information not included in the summary.

• Elaboration Seeker, who seeks elaboration by asking other members to relate the material being learned to earlier material and to other things they know.

• Memory Helper, who seeks clever ways of remembering the important ideas and facts by using drawings, mental pictures, and other memory aids and shares them with the group.

• Understanding Checker, who asks group members to explain, step-by-step, the reasoning used to complete the work, thereby making students' reasoning overt and open to correction and discussion.

• Help Seeker, who chooses someone to provide help to groupmates, asks clear and precise questions, and persists until help is given.

• Explainer, who describes how to complete the task (without giving the answer), gives specific feedback about the other students' work, and finishes by asking other students to describe or demonstrate how to complete the task.

• Explanation Facilitator, who asks other members to plan out loud how they would teach another student the material being studied. Planning how best to communicate the material can have important effects on the quality of reasoning strategies and retention.

Fermenting

Fermenting skills, the fourth level of cooperative skills, enable students to engage in academic controversies. Some of the most important aspects of learning take place when group members skillfully challenge each other's conclusions and reasoning (Johnson and R. Johnson 1989, 1991b). Academic controversies cause group members to "dig deeper" into the material, to assemble a rationale for their conclusions, to think more divergently about the issues, to find more information to support their positions, and to argue constructively about alternative solutions or decisions. Numerous skills are involved in academic controversies:

- Criticizing ideas without criticizing people.
- Differentiating when there is disagreement within the learning group.
- Integrating a number of different ideas into a single position.
- Asking for justification for a member's conclusion or answer.
- Extending another member's answer or conclusion by adding further information or implications.
- Probing by asking questions that lead to deeper understanding or analysis ("Would it work in this situation . . .?" "What else makes you believe . . . ?").
- Generating further answers by going beyond the first answer or conclusion and producing a number of plausible answers to choose from.
- Testing reality by checking out the group's work with the instructions, available time, and issues facing the group.

These skills help keep group members motivated to go beyond the quick answer to the highest quality one by stimulating group members' thinking and intellectual curiosity.

Typically, teachers begin with the forming skills to ensure that all group members are present and oriented toward working together. The functioning skills then assist the group in operating smoothly and building constructive relationships. The formulating skills ensure that high-quality learning takes place within the group and that the members engage in the necessary cognitive processing. The fermenting skills, which are the most complex and the most difficult to master, ensure that intellectual challenge and disagreement take place within the learning groups. These skills are most applicable to upper elementary, secondary, and post-secondary students. Primary and preschool students will need simplified versions of them. It's important that teachers translate cooperative skills into language and images that their students can understand and identify with. For example, the fermenting skills could be simplified to skills such as adding an idea, asking for proof, and seeing the idea from the other person's point of view (Johnson 1991, 1993; Johnson and F. Johnson 1994).

Teaching Cooperative Skills: An Example

John Dougan, in his 11th grade English class in Suffern, New York, begins a unit on grammar by teaching students a set of leadership skills. He structures positive interdependence by giving students the assignment of mastering the leadership skills and ensuring that all members of their group master the skills. The leadership roles he teaches include:

• Direction Giver, who directs the group's work by (1) reviewing instructions and restating the purpose of the assignment, (2) calling attention to time limits, and (3) offering procedures for most effectively completing the assignment.

• Summarizer, who summarizes out loud what has just been read or discussed as completely as possible from memory.

• Generator, who creates additional answers by going beyond the group members' first answers or conclusion and producing a number of plausible answers to choose from.

Dougan uses the following process to teach the leadership skills. First, he explains the skills. Second, he models the skills through demonstration. Third, he asks the class to generate a series of phrases that could be used to engage in the skills, such as "One way we could do this is. . . ." or "Another answer is . . . ." Fourth, he selects three students to roleplay for the class a group session using the skills. After the roleplay the whole class discusses each of the skills. Fifth, he has students complete the first grammar assignment using the skills as frequently as possible.

Dougan structures individual accountability by observing each group to verify that each member engages in at least two of the three targeted leadership skills. He circulates throughout the room, systematically observing each group and recording how frequently he sees students in each leadership role. Dougan structures positive reward independence by giving groups in which each member engages in at least two of the leadership behaviors five bonus points on the first grammar assignment.

The Teacher's Role

One of the most important aspects of conducting cooperative learning lessons is identifying the students who are having difficulty working effectively because of missing or underdeveloped cooperative skills. The teacher's monitoring role highlights the importance of gathering data on students as they work and intervening to encourage more appropriate behavior. Family background, role models, and the nature of the student's peer group all influence the development of social skills. The exciting part of teaching students to be more effective working with others is that the students not only gain a valuable set of skills for life, but have an excellent chance of raising their achievement as well.

As we have stated, learning cooperative skills is first of all procedural learning, very similar to learning how to play tennis or golf, perform brain surgery, or fly an airplane. Being skilled in managing conflicts involves more than simply reading material for a recognition-level or even a total-recall-level of mastery. It requires learning a procedure made up of a series of actions. Procedural learning exists when individuals:

• Learn conceptually what a skill is and when it should be used.

• Translate their conceptual understanding into a set of operational procedures (phrases and actions) appropriate for the people they are interacting with.

• Actually engage in the skill.

• Eliminate errors by moving through the phases of skill mastery.

• Attain a routine-use, automatic level of mastery.

Procedural learning involves breaking a complex process into its component parts and then systematically learning the process until it becomes automatic. It differs from simply learning facts and acquiring knowledge by relying heavily on feedback about performance and modifying one's implementation until the errors of performance are eliminated. It's a gradual process—one's efforts to perform the skill will fail to match the ideal of what one wishes to accomplish for a considerable length of time. Failure is part of the process of gaining expertise, and success is inevitable when failure is followed by persistent practice, feedback, and reflection on how to perform the skill more competently.

Gaining expertise requires "learning partners" who are willing to trust each other, talk frankly, and observe each other's performance over a prolonged period of time to identify the errors being made in implementing the skill. Unless students are willing to reveal a lack of expertise to obtain accurate feedback, expertise cannot be gained. In other words, procedural learning, and the mastery of all skills, requires cooperation among students and the security to try and fail and try again.

There are five major steps in teaching cooperative skills:

• Ensuring that students *see the need* for the skill.

• Ensuring that students *understand* what the skill is and when it should be used.

• Setting up *practice* situations and encouraging mastery of the skill.

• Ensuring that students have the time and the needed *procedures for processing* (and receiving feedback on) how well they are using the skill.

• Ensuring that students *persevere* in practicing the skill until it becomes a natural action.

Step 1: Helping Students See the Need for the Skill. To be motivated to learn cooperative skills, students must believe that they will be better off knowing the skills. Teachers can promote students' awareness of the need for cooperative skills by:

• Displaying posters, bulletin boards, and other evidence that they consider the skills important. It's often easy to see what is important in a classroom by looking at the walls, boards, and seating arrangements.

• Communicating to students why mastering the skills is important. With many students, sharing information about the need for cooperative skills in career and family settings is enough. Other students may benefit from experiencing how the skills help them do better work.

• Validating the importance of the skills by assigning a grade or giving a reward to groups whose members demonstrate competence in the skills. Many teachers give learning groups two grades: one for achievement and one for the appropriate use of targeted cooperative skills.

Step 2: Ensuring that Students Understand the Skill. To learn a skill, students must have a clear idea of what the skill is and how to perform it. There is little chance of being too concrete in defining cooperative skills. *First,* a clear, operational definition of the *skill must be developed.* Students must understand what the skill is and when it should be used. This is most commonly done through a "T-Chart" (see Figure 8.1 on page 72) (Johnson, Johnson, and Holubec 1992) and through modeling the skill. A teacher can list the skill on the T-Chart (e.g., encouraging participation) and ask the class, *"What would this skill look like?"* After several nonverbal behaviors are generated, the teacher can ask the class, *"What would this skill sound like?"* After several phrases have been listed, the T-Chart can be prominently displayed for reference.

FIGURE 8.1
Encouraging Participation
T-Chart

Looks Like	Sounds Like
Smiles	What's your idea?
Eye Contact	Awesome!
Thumbs Up	Good idea!
Pat on Back	That's interesting.

Second, the skill is demonstrated and modeled until the students have a clear idea of what the skill sounds and looks like. It may help to have students roleplay the skill or to set up a short counterexample where the skill is obviously missing.

It's important not to try to teach too many skills at the same time. It's best to start with one or two. One 1st grade curriculum unit we have helped with teaches eight skills over a year's time, starting with "Everyone Does a Job," and including "Sharing Ideas and Materials," "Giving Directions Without Being Bossy," and "Caring About Others' Feelings."

Step 3: Setting Up Repetitive Practice Situations. To master a skill, students need to repeatedly practice it. Students should be asked to roleplay a skill several times with the person sitting next to them immediately after the skill is defined. An initial practice session should be long enough for the skill to be fairly well learned by each student, and then short practice sessions should be structured over several days or weeks. As students practice, teachers should continue to give verbal instructions and encourage students to perform the skills with proper sequence and timing. Some of the strategies for encouraging practice include:

• Assigning specific roles to group members to ensure that they practice the skills. A teacher can assign the roles of reader, encourager, summarizer, and elaboration seeker to the members of a cooperative learning group. The roles can be rotated daily until every student has been responsible for each role several times.

• Announcing that the occurrence of the skills will be observed. It's surprising how much practice occurs when a teacher announces that she will be looking for a specific skill and stands next to a group with an observation sheet. The teacher's presence and the knowledge that the frequency of the skills is being counted and valued by the teacher (or a student observer) are potent motivators.

• Using nonacademic skill-building exercises to provide students with a chance to practice cooperative skills. At times, a fun exercise that is not part of the ongoing classwork can be used to encourage students to practice specific skills. Many such exercises have been used successfully (see Johnson 1991, 1993; Johnson and F. Johnson 1994; Johnson and R. Johnson 1994).

Because new skills need to be cued consistently and reinforced for some time, teachers should be relentless in encouraging prolonged use of cooperative skills.

Step 4: Ensuring that Students Process Their Use of the Skills. Practicing cooperative skills is not enough. Students must process how frequently and how well they are using the skills. Students need to receive feedback and discuss, describe, and reflect on their use of the skills to improve their performances. To ensure that students do this, teachers need to provide a regular time for group processing and give students group processing procedures to follow. A standard processing task is, "Name three things your group did well and one thing your group could do even better next time." Such group processing not only increases students' interpersonal and small-group skills, but also increases achievement (Johnson, Johnson, Stanne, and Garibaldi 1990; Yager, Johnson, and Johnson 1985) and the quality of the relationships students develop (Putnam, Rynders, Johnson, and Johnson 1989). Teachers might have to model group processing initially and periodically so that students take it seriously and become adept at it.

The following strategies for encouraging group processing are helpful.

• Provide regular time for processing. Ten minutes at the end of each period or 20 minutes once a week are typical.

• Provide a set of procedures for students to follow. A processing sheet that the group fills out together, signs, and then hands in can be used. Questions might include, "How many members felt they had a chance to share their ideas in the group?" and "How many members felt listened to?" The most effective procedure, however, is to have one member of the group observe the frequency with which each member engages in one of the targeted skills and give each member performance feedback in the discussion at the end of the period.

• Provide opportunities for positive feedback among group members. One way to do this is to have each member tell every other member one action that reflected effective use of a cooperative skill.

Step 5: Ensuring that Students Persevere in Practicing the Skills. With most skills there is a period of slow learning, then a period of rapid improvement, then a period where performance remains about the same, then another period of rapid improvement, then another plateau, and so forth. Students have to practice cooperative skills long enough to make it through the first few plateaus and integrate the skills into their behavioral repertoires. Most skill development goes through the following stages:

1. Awareness that the skill is needed.
2. Understanding of what the skill is.
3. Self-conscious, awkward engagement in the skill. (Practicing any new skill feels awkward at first).
4. Feelings of phoniness while engaging in the skill. (Many students feel unauthentic or phony while initially using a skill. After a while the awkwardness passes and enacting the skill becomes smoother. Teacher and peer encouragement are needed to move students through this stage.)
5. Skilled but mechanical use of the skill.
6. Automatic, routine use where the skill is fully integrated into a person's behavioral repertoire and seems like a natural action.

Ways to ensure that students persevere include continuing to assign the skill as a group role, continuing to give students feedback about how frequently and how well they are performing the skill, and reinforcing the groups when members use the skill. We have found that students (even socially isolated and withdrawn students) learn more social skills and engage in them more frequently when the group is given bonus points for their efforts (Lew, Mesch, Johnson, and Johnson 1986a, 1986b).

If the potential of cooperative learning is to be realized, students must have the prerequisite interpersonal and small-group skills and be motivated to use them. These skills need to be taught just as systematically as academic content. Doing so involves communicating to students the need for the social skills, defining and modeling the skills, having students practice the skills over and over again, processing how effectively the students are performing the skills, and ensuring that students persevere until the skills are fully integrated into their behavioral repertoires. Doing so will not only increase student achievement, it will also increase students' future employability, career success, relationship quality, and psychological health.

Nothing we learn is more important than the skills required to work cooperatively with other people. Most human interaction is cooperative. Without some skill in cooperating effectively, it is difficult (if not impossible) to maintain a marriage, hold a job, or be part of any community. We have only discussed a few of the interpersonal and small-group skills needed for effective cooperation. A more thorough and extensive coverage of these skills can be found in *Reaching Out* (Johnson 1993), *Joining Together* (Johnson and F. Johnson 1994), *Human Relations and Your Career* (Johnson 1991), and *Learning Together and Alone* (Johnson and R. Johnson 1975/1991a).

9

Cooperation and Conflict

Cooperation and conflict go hand-in-hand. Conflicts among group members are inevitable once cooperative learning is established in the classroom and faculty collegial support groups have been established in the school (see Chapter 10). The absence of conflict is often a sign of apathy and indifference, not harmony. The more group members care about achieving the group's goals and about each other, the more likely conflicts are to arise. Managed constructively, conflicts are an essential and valuable source of creativity, fun, higher-level reasoning, and effective decision making. Managed destructively, however, they are a source of divisiveness, anger, frustration, and failure. Students and faculty need to learn procedures for effectively managing conflicts and to become skillful in their use.

Students often have procedures for managing conflicts, but the procedures are not always constructive or shared among all classmates. One student may use physical violence, another may use verbal violence, another may withdraw, and a fourth may try to persuade. The presence of multiple procedures creates some chaos. This is especially evident with students from different cultural, ethnic, social class, and language backgrounds. Thus, it is important that *all* students (and staff members) learn to use the same set of conflict management procedures. Teaching these procedures involves establishing a cooperative context, showing students how to engage in academic controversies constructively, and establishing a peer mediation program in the classroom and school (see Johnson and Johnson 1989a, 1991b, 1992d).

FIGURE 9.1

M A N A G I N G

Create a Cooperative Environment

Structure Academic Controversies.
Teach Procedure and Skills.

C O N F L I C T

Structure Peacemaking Program.
Teach Negotiation and Mediation
Procedures and Skills.
Arbitrate as a Last Resort.

Establishing a Cooperative Context

The best way I know how to defeat an enemy is to make him a friend.
—Abraham Lincoln

A cooperative context must be established if conflicts are to be resolved constructively. The more participants in a conflict recognize and value their long-term mutual interests, perceive their interdependence, and are invested in each other's well-being, the easier it is to resolve conflicts constructively. Teachers can best establish a cooperative classroom environment by using cooperative learning the majority of each day.

Engaging in Academic Controversy

It's best that we should not all think alike. It's difference of opinion that makes horse races.
—Mark Twain

In their social studies class, students are considering the issue of civil disobedience. They learn that in the civil rights movement, individuals broke the law to gain equal rights for minorities. They learn that in numerous instances, such as the civil rights and antiwar movements, individuals wrestled with the issue of breaking the law to redress social injustice. In the past few years, however, prominent public figures from Wall Street to the White House have felt justified in breaking laws for personal or political gain. In order to study the role of civil disobedience in a democracy, the students are placed in cooperative learning groups. Each group is then divided into two pairs. One pair is given the assignment of making the best case possible for the constructiveness of civil disobedience in a democracy. The other pair is given the assignment of making the best case possible for the destructiveness of civil disobedience in a democracy. In the resulting conflict, students draw from such sources as the Declaration of Independence by Thomas Jefferson, *Civil Disobedience* by Henry David Thoreau, "Speech at Cooper Union, New York" by Abraham Lincoln, and "Letter from Birmingham Jail" by Martin

Luther King, Jr., to challenge each others' reasoning and analyses concerning when civil disobedience is, or is not, constructive.

Controversy exists when one student's ideas, information, conclusions, theories, and opinions are incompatible with another student's, and the two seek to reach an agreement. Controversies are resolved through what Aristotle called *deliberate discourse* (i.e., the discussion of the advantages and disadvantages of proposed actions) aimed at synthesizing novel solutions (i.e., creative problem solving). In an academic controversy, students engage in the following steps (Johnson and Johnson 1977, 1992a):

1. *Research and Prepare a Position.* Students are divided into pairs. Each pair develops the position assigned, learns the relevant information, and plans how to present the best case possible to the other pair. Near the end of the period each pair is encouraged to compare notes with pairs from other groups who represent the same position.

2. *Present and Advocate Their Position.* Each pair makes their presentation to the opposing pair. Both members of each pair must participate in the presentation. Students are to be as persuasive and convincing as possible. Members of the opposing pair are encouraged to take notes, listen carefully to learn the information being presented, and clarify anything they do not understand.

3. *Refute Opposing Positions and Rebut Attacks on Their Own.* Students argue forcefully and persuasively for their position, presenting as many facts as they can to support their claims. The group members analyze and critically evaluate the information, rationale, and inductive and deductive reasoning of the opposing pair, asking them for the facts that support their point of view. They refute the arguments of the opposing pair and rebut attacks on their position. They discuss the issue following a set of rules to help them criticize ideas without criticizing people, differentiate the two positions, and assess the degree of evidence and logic supporting each position (Johnson and Johnson 1992a). They keep in mind that the issue is complex and they need to know both sides to write a good report.

4. *Reverse Perspectives.* The pairs reverse perspectives and present each other's positions. In arguing for the opposing position, students are forceful and persuasive. They add information that the opposing pair didn't think to present. They strive to see the issue from both perspectives simultaneously.

5. *Synthesize and Integrate the Best Evidence and Reasoning into a Joint Position.* The two pairs from each group drop all advocacy and

synthesize and integrate what they know into factual, judgmental conclusions, which are summarized into a joint position to which all sides
can agree. They finalize the report (the teacher evaluates the reports on
the quality of the writing, the logical presentation of evidence, and the
oral presentation to the class); present their conclusions to the class (all
four members of the group are required to participate orally in the
presentation); individually take a test covering both sides of the issue (if
every member of the group achieves a certain criterion, they all receive
bonus points); and process how well they worked together and how they
could be even more effective next time.

As Thomas Jefferson noted, "Difference of opinion leads to inquiry,
and inquiry to truth." Such intellectual "disputed passages" create
higher achievement (characterized by critical thinking, higher-level reasoning, and metacognitive thought) when they occur within cooperative
learning groups and are carefully structured to ensure that students
manage them constructively (Johnson and Johnson 1977, 1979, 1992a).
Students who participate in an academic controversy recall more correct
information, are better able to transfer learning to new situations, and
use more complex and higher-level reasoning strategies in recalling and
transferring learned information. In problem-solving situations, controversy tends to increase the number and quality of ideas generated, the
use of a wider range of ideas, the use of more varied problem-solving
strategies, and the development of creative, imaginative, and novel
solutions. Controversy also tends to increase students' liking and social
support of one another, ability to accurately take the perspectives of
others, and academic self-esteem. Engaging in a controversy can also be
fun, enjoyable, and exciting. Samuel Johnson once stated, "I dogmatize
and am contradicted, and in this conflict of opinions and sentiments I
find delight." John Milton, in *Doctrine and Discipline*, stated "Where
there is much desire to learn, there of necessity will be much arguing,
much writing, many opinions; for opinion in good men is but knowledge
in the making."

When engaged in academic controversies, individual students go
through five separate cognitive stages as they work cooperatively to
move from their initial individual hypotheses about a situation or
question to the final position that is supported by their group (Johnson
and Johnson 1979, 1992a). First, when students are presented with an
issue or problem, they have an initial conclusion based on categorizing
and organizing their current information and experiences and their

specific perspectives. Second, when asked to present their conclusion and its rationale to others, students engage in cognitive rehearsal, conceptually reorganize the rationale for their position as they present it, deepen their understanding of their position, and find themselves using higher-level reasoning strategies. Third, as classmates present opposing positions (based on their information, experiences, and perspectives), the intellectual "disputed passage" causes students to become uncertain as to the correctness of their views, resulting in a state of conceptual conflict or disequilibrium. Fourth, the more uncertain students become, the more motivated they are to actively search for more information, new experiences, and a more adequate perspective. Berlyne calls this active search "epistemic curiosity." Like Macbeth, who said, "Stay, you imperfect speakers, tell me more," students want more information. In their search for it, divergent attention and thoughts are stimulated and a higher-level reasoning process is sought in hopes of resolving the uncertainty. Finally, students resolve their uncertainty by accommodating the perspective and reasoning of others and developing a new, reconceptualized, and reorganized conclusion. As Andre Gide said, "One completely overcomes only what one assimilates." Novel solutions and decisions are detected, which are, on balance, qualitatively better. This process can be repeated to promote even greater learning and understanding. Hundreds of studies validate this posited process (Johnson and Johnson 1989a). Perhaps it is this process that Edmund Burke had in mind when he said, "He that wrestles with us strengthens our nerves, and sharpens our skill. Our antagonist is our helper."

Establishing a Peer Mediation Program

Teaching Students To Be Peacemakers (Johnson and Johnson 1991b) is a curriculum that can be used to help students resolve their own conflicts and mediate their classmates' conflicts. In cooperative teams, individuals' wants, needs, values, and goals often conflict. Two students may both want to use a book or a computer. Two others may both want to be first in line. When such conflicts-of-interests occur, settlements must be negotiated. A peacemaker program can be used to teach students the procedures and skills they need to manage conflicts-of-interests constructively. Establishing the program involves three steps: teaching students to resolve their own conflicts, teaching students to mediate their classmates' conflicts, and implementing the program.

Teaching Students To Resolve Their Own Conflicts

The first step in establishing a peacemaker program is to teach *all* students to negotiate constructive resolutions to their own conflicts. Students need to both understand the negotiation procedure and have the skills required to use it. The procedure and skills need to be overlearned so they are available for use when emotions run high and feelings such as fear and anger are intense. Even under such conditions, students need to be able to follow the negotiation procedures. They must define their conflict, exchange positions and proposals, view the situation from both perspectives, invent options for mutual gain, and reach a wise agreement. To do this, students must be taught the following procedure (Johnson and Johnson 1991b, 1991c):

1. State what you want: "I want to use the book now."
2. State how you feel: "I'm frustrated."
3. State the reasons for your wants and feelings: "You've been using the book for the past hour. If I don't get to use the book soon my report will not be done on time. It's frustrating to have to wait so long."
4. Summarize your understanding of what the other person wants, how the other person feels, and the reasons underlying both.
5. Invent three optional plans to resolve the conflict.
6. Choose one of the plans and shake hands.

Teaching Students To Mediate Their Classmates' Conflicts

The second step in establishing the peacemaker program is to teach *all* students how to mediate constructive resolutions of their classmates' conflicts. When students cannot successfully negotiate a constructive resolution of their own conflicts, peer mediators should be available to them. *Mediation* is the use of the services of another person to help settle a dispute. All students should be taught how to mediate constructive resolutions of their classmates' conflicts by introducing the mediation process, presenting the guidelines and the rules for mediation, assisting the participants through the negotiation sequence, and finalizing the agreement. Students should be taught the following *mediation procedure* (Johnson and Johnson 1987, 1991b, 1991c):

The mediator introduces himself and the process of mediation. He asks if both students want to solve the problem and does not proceed until they answer "yes." The mediator explains the guidelines by stating: "Mediation is voluntary. My role is to help you find a solution to your conflict that is acceptable to both of you. I am neutral. I will not take sides or attempt to decide who is right or wrong. I will help you decide how to solve the conflict. Each person will have the chance to state his or her view of the conflict without interruption."

The mediator then explains the rules: "The rules are that you must agree to solve the problem, not resort to name calling, not interrupt, be as honest as you can, abide by any solutions you agree upon, and keep anything said in mediation confidential. I will also not tell anyone what is said."

He next takes the two participants through the steps of negotiation. Participants discuss what they want, how they feel, and their reasons; they reverse perspectives, generate three optional agreements, and finally they reach a mutually acceptable agreement. The mediator then becomes the keeper of the agreement and checks in periodically to make sure the agreement is working. If not, the mediation process is repeated.

Implementing the Program

The third step in establishing the peacemaker program is its implementation by the teacher. Students receive 30 minutes of training each day for thirty days using the curriculum *Teaching Students To Be Peacemakers* (Johnson and Johnson 1991b). Students roleplay and practice the procedures and skills involved in negotiating and mediating until they can negotiate and mediate at a routine-use level.

Once the initial training is complete, the program is implemented. Each day the teacher selects two class members to serve as official class mediators. They are responsible for helping classmates resolve any conflicts they cannot negotiate a wise agreement to themselves. They wear official t-shirts and patrol the playground and lunchroom. The role of mediator should be rotated so that each student serves an equal amount of time. Refresher lessons are taught once or twice a week to refine students' negotiation and mediation skills.

The Last Resort

Negotiation and mediation are self-empowering—they enable students to make decisions about issues and conflicts that affect their own lives rather than having a decision imposed on them by teachers and administrators. This does not mean, however, that students will always be able to resolve their conflicts constructively. When negotiation and mediation fail, the teacher or principal must arbitrate. *Arbitration* is the submission of a dispute to a disinterested third party who makes a final and binding judgment as to how the conflict will be resolved.

Peacemaking and Discipline Problems

Discipline problems plague classrooms and schools. Students often bicker, threaten, tease, and harass each other. Conflicts involving racial and cultural differences are increasing. Violence is escalating. Truancy is epidemic. And these problems consume considerable teacher and administrator time.

Classroom and school discipline programs may be classified on a continuum from those based on external rewards and punishments that control and manage student behavior to those based on teaching students the competencies and skills required to resolve their interpersonal conflicts constructively, cope with stress and adversity, and behave in appropriate and constructive ways. At one end of the continuum the focus is on the faculty and staff controlling and managing student behavior. At the other end of the continuum the focus is on students regulating their own actions and helping their peers to do the same.

Most discipline programs are clustered at the "adult administering external rewards and punishment" end of the continuum. Thus, it is up to the staff to monitor student behavior, determine whether it is or is not within the bounds of acceptability, and force students to terminate inappropriate actions. When the infractions are minor, the staff often arbitrate ("The pencil belongs to Mary. Jane, be quiet and sit down.") or cajole students to end hostilities ("Let's forgive and forget. Shake hands and be friends.") If that doesn't work, students may be sent to the principal's office for a stern but cursory lecture about the value of getting along, a threat that if the conflict continues more drastic action will ensue, and a final admonition to "Go and fight no more." Time-out rooms are also used. Eventually, some students are even expelled from school. Such programs cost a great deal in instructional and administrative time and work only as long as students are under surveillance. They teach students that adult authority figures are needed to resolve conflicts. They do not empower students. Adults may become more skillful in how to control students, but students do not learn the procedures, skills, and attitudes required to resolve conflicts constructively in their own personal lives at home, in school, at work, and in the community.

At the other end of the continuum are programs aimed at teaching students self-responsibility and self-regulation. Self-regulation is the ability to act in socially accepted ways in the absence of external monitors; the ability to initiate and cease activities according to situational demands. Self-regulation is a central and significant hallmark of cognitive and social development. To regulate their own behavior, students must monitor that behavior, assess situations, consider other people's perspectives when making judgments as to which behaviors are appropriate, and master the procedures and skills required to engage in the desired behavior. This is the only way students can learn to act appropriately and competently.

If students are to learn how to regulate their behavior, they must have opportunities to (1) make decisions regarding how to behave and (2) follow through on those decisions. Allowing students to do so, to be joint architects in matters affecting them, promotes feelings of control and autonomy. Students who can manage their conflicts constructively and regulate their own behavior certainly have a developmental advantage over those who cannot. The peer mediation program teaches all students the joint problem-solving and decision-making competencies and skills they need to regulate their own and their classmates' behavior. Ideally, students are given this responsibility so that teachers can concentrate on instruction rather than control.

❦   ❦   ❦

With cooperation comes conflict. How such conflict is managed largely determines the success of cooperative efforts. In order to ensure that conflict is constructive, teachers must establish a cooperative context in the classroom and school, teach students how to manage intellectual conflicts inherent in learning groups through academic controversy, and teach students to negotiate constructive resolutions of their own and their classmates' conflicts through the peacemaking process. By helping students manage their conflicts constructively, student learning and the quality of life within the school are increased, and students are empowered to regulate their own behavior and deal with adversity in their lives.

The *Tao Te Ching* states, "By blending the breath of the sun and the shade, true harmony comes into the world." Cooperation may be seen as the sun and conflict as the shade. These two go hand-in-hand.

10

The Cooperative School

The issue of cooperation among students is part of a larger issue of the organizational structure of schools (Johnson and Johnson 1989b). The organizational structure of any school reflects the school system to which it belongs and basic assumptions about how students learn and how they should be instructed. Many schools are in the process of changing from mass-production organizational structures to team-based organizational structures. The team-based structure is known as the cooperative school, which involves the use of cooperative learning in the classroom, faculty collegial support groups in the school, a school-based decision-making structure, and faculty meetings predominated by cooperative procedures. The heart of the cooperative school is the collegial teaching team, whose focus is the continuous improvement of teacher expertise in using cooperative learning.

The Cooperative School Structure

Willi Unsoeld, a renowned mountain climber and philosopher, once stated, "Take care of each other, share your energies with the group, no one must feel alone, cut off, for that is when you do not make it." This thought applies to everyone in schools. For nearly a century, teachers have worked alone, in their own rooms, with their own students, and with their own curriculum materials. Students have been randomly assigned to teachers because teachers have been believed to be equivalent and, therefore, can be given any student to teach.

In order for schools to focus on the quality of instruction, they need to successfully change from this mass-production competitive/individualistic organizational structure to a high-performance, cooperative, team-based organizational structure (see Johnson and Johnson 1989b). They need to develop the cooperative school. Retraining teachers to use cooperative learning while organizing teachers to mass produce educated students is self-defeating. W. Edwards Deming and others have suggested that more than 85 percent of all the things that go wrong in any organization are directly attributable to the organization's structure, not the nature of the individuals involved. Changing teaching methods is much easier when the changes are congruent with (not in opposition to) the organizational structure of the school, which, in turn, must be congruent with the overall school system.

In a cooperative school structure, students work primarily in cooperative learning groups, and teachers and building staff work in cooperative teams, as do district administrators (Johnson and Johnson 1989b). The organizational structure of the classroom, school, and district are thus congruent. Effective teamwork is the very center of improving the quality of instruction and education with each level of cooperative teams supporting and enhancing the other levels. Teamwork is the hub around which all other elements of school improvement revolve. Teams are, beyond all doubt, the most direct sources of continuous improvement of instruction and education.

Contributing to team efforts is becoming paramount at every level in modern organizations. Schools are no exception. Students and faculty have to want to belong to teams, they must contribute their share of the work, and they must take positions and know how to advocate their views in ways that spark creative problem solving. The student or educator who doesn't pull with peers will increasingly be the odd person out.

The Cooperative Classroom

The first level of a cooperative school structure is the classroom where cooperative learning is used for the majority of the instructional time (Johnson and Johnson 1989b) (see Figure 10.1 on page 88). Work teams are the heart of the team-based organizational structure and cooperative learning groups form the primary work teams. Quality learning results from a team effort to challenge each other's reasoning and maximize each other's learning. Cooperative learning increases student achievement, creates more positive relationships among students, and generally improves students' psychological well-being. Cooperative learning is also the prerequisite and foundation for most other instructional innovations, including thematic curriculum, whole language, critical thinking, active reading, process writing, materials-based (problem-solving) mathematics, and learning communities. In addition, cooperative learning affects teachers' attitudes and competencies regarding working collaboratively because what is promoted during instructional time tends to dominate relationships among staff members.

The Cooperative School

The second level in creating a cooperative school structure is to form collegial teaching teams, task forces, and ad hoc decision-making groups within the school (Johnson and Johnson 1989b). The use of cooperative learning in the classroom occurs most effectively when staff work in collegial teaching teams, faculty meetings are structured cooperatively, and school-based decision making takes place within a cooperative context.

FIGURE 10.1
The Cooperative School

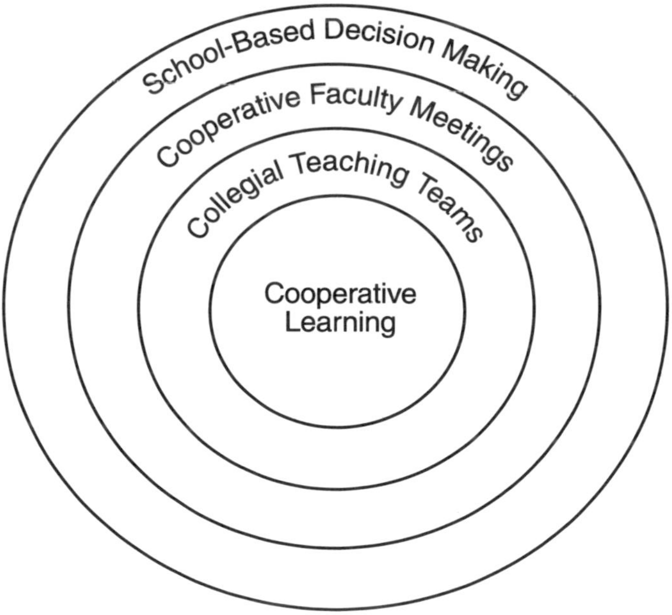

Collegial teaching teams. Just as cooperative learning is at the heart of the classroom, the collegial teaching team is at the heart of the school. *Collegial teaching teams* are small, cooperative groups (from two to five faculty members) whose purpose is to increase teachers' instructional expertise and success (Johnson and Johnson 1989b). The focus is on improving instruction in general and increasing members' expertise in using cooperative learning in particular. Collegial teams are first and foremost safe places where members like to be; where there is support, caring, concern, laughter, camaraderie, and celebration; and where the primary goal of continually improving each other's competence in using cooperative learning is never obscured.

As we've said, in mass-production schools, teachers are isolated from each other and may feel alienated, overloaded, harried, and over-whelmed. This isolation and alienation is reduced when teachers form collegial teaching teams. Teachers generally teach better when they work in collegial teaching teams to jointly support each other's efforts to increase their instructional expertise. Collegial teaching teams give teachers ownership of the professional agenda, break down the barriers to collegial interaction, and reduce program fragmentation. Collegial teaching teams undertake three key activities (Johnson and Johnson 1989b.

• *Frequent professional discussions of cooperative learning.* Collegial interaction is essential for building collaborative cultures in schools (Little 1990) and critical for teachers' ongoing professional development (Nias 1984). Expertise in using cooperative learning begins with conceptual understanding of the nature of cooperative learning, how to implement cooperative learning, and what results can be expected from using cooperative learning. Teachers must also think critically about the strategy and adapt it to their specific students and subject areas. In team discussions, teachers consolidate and strengthen their knowledge about cooperative learning and provide each other with relevant feedback about the degree to which mastery and understanding have been achieved. Within collegial teams, faculty members exchange understandings of what cooperative learning is and how it may be used within their classes. They develop a common vocabulary, share information, celebrate successes, and solve implementation problems.

• *Co-planning, co-designing, and co-preparing cooperative learning lessons and instructional units.* Once teachers understand cooperative learning, they must implement it. Members of collegial teams should frequently design, prepare, and evaluate lesson plans together. Doing so distributes the work of developing the materials and machinery for implementing cooperative learning. Integrated curriculum and thematic teaching clearly depend on co-planning and co-designing.

• *Co-teaching cooperative lessons and jointly processing observations.* If faculty are to progress through the initial awkward and mechanical stages to mastering the use of cooperative learning, they must receive continual feedback about the accuracy of their implementation and be encouraged to persevere in their implementation attempts long enough to integrate cooperative learning into their ongoing instructional practice. The more time colleagues spend involved in each other's teaching, the more valuable the help and assistance they can provide. Frequently co-teaching cooperative lessons and then providing each other with useful feedback provides members of collegial teams with shared experiences to discuss and reflect upon, thus promoting continuous improvement.

Collegial teams ideally meet daily. At a minimum, teams should meet weekly. During a typical meeting team members review how they have used cooperative learning since the previous meeting, share a success in doing so, complete a quality chart (see page 98) on their implementation of cooperative learning, set three to five goals to accomplish before the next meeting, decide how they will help each other achieve their goals, learn something new about cooperative learning, and celebrate (Johnson and Johnson 1989b). Following this agenda ensures that teachers (1) experience the learning environment they are creating for students (i.e., they meet with supportive peers who encourage them to learn and grow), (2) have a procedure for continuously improving their use of cooperative learning, (3) receive continuous training in how to use cooperative learning, (4) encourage pride of workmanship and recognize and celebrate self-improvement (i.e., any time a faculty member makes an effort to improve, the effort can be recognized and celebrated by teammates), and (5) discourage poor workmanship and negativism.

Task forces and ad hoc decision-making groups. School-based decision making occurs through the use of two types of cooperative teams: task forces and ad hoc decision-making groups (Johnson and Johnson 1989b). Task forces plan and implement solutions to schoolwide issues and problems such as curriculum adoptions and lunchroom behavior. Task forces diagnose a problem, gather data about the causes and extent of the problem, consider a variety of alternative solutions, make conclusions, and present a recommendation to the faculty as a whole. Ad hoc decision-making groups are part of a small-group/large-group procedure in which staff members as a whole listen to a recommendation, are assigned to small groups, meet to consider the recommendation, report to the entire faculty their decision, and then participate in a whole-faculty decision as to what the course of action should be. The use of these two types of faculty cooperative teams tends to increase teacher productivity, morale, and professional self-esteem.

The clearest modeling of cooperative procedures in the school may be in faculty meetings and other meetings structured by the school administration. When administrators use a competitive/individualistic format of lecture, whole-group discussion, and individual worksheets in faculty meetings, they make a powerful statement about the way they want their faculty to teach. Formal and informal cooperative groups, cooperative base groups, and repetitive structures can be used during faculty meetings just as they can be used within the classroom, thus making faculty meetings staff development and training as well as business meetings.

The Cooperative District

The third level of a cooperative school structure is administrative cooperative teams within the district (Johnson and Johnson 1989b). Administrators should be organized into collegial teams, task forces, and ad hoc triads (temporary groups of three) as part of the shared decision-making process. Using cooperative procedures during administrative meetings is the best way to model what the school district should be like. If administrators compete to see who is the best administrator in the district, they aren't likely to promote cooperation among staff members at the schools. The more the district and school personnel work in cooperative teams, the easier it is for teachers to envision and use cooperative learning, and vice versa.

Quality Education in the Cooperative School

In the mass-production school, teachers are primarily organized on a horizontal basis (grade level or departmental teams). Students are sent from work station to work station to be partially educated (e.g., from math class to science class to social studies class, or from 1st grade to 2nd grade to 3rd grade) with each teacher responsible for a small part of the student's education. Barriers separate teachers, forcing each to focus full attention on only a small piece of the overall program.

In the cooperative school, teams are not an option. They are a given. All important work is done by teams. The primary faculty team, the collegial teaching team, focuses on instruction and teaching. Teachers are formed into vertical (cross-disciplinary) teams with a number of teachers responsible for the same students for a number of years. Vertical teams break down the barriers that separate teachers, grade levels, and academic departments and ensure that all teachers see the overall process toward which their efforts are contributing. An elementary team may be made up of two primary and two secondary teachers who are given responsibility for educating about 120 students for 6 years. A secondary team may be made up of an English, math, science, social studies, and foreign language teacher, who are given responsibility for educating 120 students for 3 years (for example, from 7th through 9th grades).

Vertical teams use integrated curriculum and thematic teaching. Each team is genuinely accountable because it has the same students for several years. No one can blame a student's deficiencies in reading or math on last year's teacher or just mark time with problem students until they are passed on to the next teacher. Teachers have to confront difficulties and live with the consequences of their decisions. But, because they are part of a team, they need never face those challenges alone.

Organizing teachers into vertical teaching teams creates a setting that focuses on the quality of education in the school. The notion of quality education is loosely based on W. Edwards Deming's fourteen points (Walton 1986). A set of guidelines for achieving quality education in the cooperative school can be established from Deming's recommendations for achieving quality education.

A constancy of purpose must be established within the school through clarifying and highlighting the overall positive goal interdependence. Faculty and staff must believe that they sink or swim together. They must perceive that they are responsible not only for improving their own expertise, but also for improving the expertise of every other person in the school. Faculty and staff must agree upon a set of overall goals that highlights their interdependence and the need for a joint effort. These goals should reflect a new definition of the school that focuses attention *not* on standardized test scores, but on the continuous improvement of the quality of instruction.

The school must adopt the philosophy that faculty teams must successfully educate and socialize every student placed in their care. No failures to educate or graduate are acceptable. Instead of being tolerant of mistakes and failures, teachers must ensure that every student is educated and socialized. When teachers work with the same students for a number of years, they can provide the support and problem solving that result in every student learning, graduating, and going on to post-secondary education.

Instead of relying on mass standardized testing to achieve quality, educators must focus on improving the instructional process. Inspection is unnecessary if every faculty member is committed to quality instruction.

Fear must be driven out of the school so faculty can take risks to increase their competence. Anything that causes humiliation, self-defense, or fear in a school is destructive. The major source of fear within schools is competition and the extrinsic motivation it promotes. Ranking teachers from highest to lowest and giving merit pay on a normative basis all create anxiety, evaluation apprehension, and fear. Driving out fear requires more than simply saying, "Do not compete." The social support and positive relationships in cooperative teams reduce fear and provide the security teachers need to change, grow, and cooperate.

Faculty must develop strong personal relationships with students. Faculty must stay "close to the customer" for at least two reasons—to obtain the information needed to provide quality education and to motivate students to do their best. Schools have a number of clients, including parents, the community, our society, employers, and post-secondary educational institutions. The most direct clients of schools, however, are students. To influence students to commit energy to learning, faculty members must build caring relationships with students that prove their commitment to students' well being and success. Long-term, committed efforts to succeed come from the heart, not the head, and relationships are the fastest way to the heart (Johnson and Johnson 1989b).

Faculty must persistently strive to reduce waste in the instructional system and school. Reducing waste is an essential aspect of increasing quality within an organization. Integrating the curriculum and thematic teaching, for example, help reduce the redundancy among subject areas.

Continuous Improvement

To have joy one must share it. Happiness was born a twin.
—Indian Proverb

For a school to be successful, everyone in it must be dedicated to continuous improvement. In Japan, this mutual dedication is called *kaizen*, a societywide covenant of mutual help in the process of getting better and better, day by day. Schools must commit the resources necessary for *kaizen* to occur. These resources include eliminating all competition among teachers and students, structuring cooperation at all levels of the school, focusing faculty's attention on daily improvement of cooperative learning and other aspects of instruction, and providing the time for faculty collegial teaching teams to meet.

The professional discussions, co-planning, and co-teaching that occur in collegial teaching groups are aimed at continuous improvement through progressive refinement of expertise in cooperative learning. Faculty progressively refine their competence in using cooperative learning by (1) understanding conceptually what cooperative learning is and how it can be implemented, (2) trying it out in their classrooms, (3) assessing how well their cooperative learning lessons worked, and (4) reflecting on what they did, modifying their plans, and trying again in an improved way (Johnson and Johnson 1989b). Let's look more closely at each of these steps.

1. *Understand what cooperative learning is and how it can be implemented in the classroom.* Teachers must understand the five essential components of effective cooperation and the their role in using formal and informal cooperative learning and cooperative base groups. Approaches to using cooperative learning may be ordered on a continuum from conceptual/adaptive approaches (using general conceptual models to plan and tailor cooperative learning specifically for a teacher's circumstances, students, and needs) to direct/prescriptive approaches (prepackaged lessons, curriculums, strategies, and activities used in a lock-step, prescribed manner). Conceptual approaches train teachers to be engineers in their use of cooperative learning, while direct approaches train teachers to be technicians. Engineers conceptually understand cooperative learning and, therefore, can adapt it to their specific teaching circumstances, students, and curriculums and repair it when it doesn't work. Technicians are trained to teach pre-packaged lessons, curricu-

lums, and strategies in a lock-step, prescribed manner without really understanding what cooperation is or what makes it work.

The conceptual (engineer) approach is used in all technological arts and crafts. An engineer designing a bridge, for example, applies validated theory to the unique problems imposed by the need for a bridge of a certain length, to carry specific loads, from a bank of one unique geological character to a bank of another unique geological character, in an area with specific winds, temperatures, and susceptibility to earthquakes. The conceptual approach to cooperative learning requires teachers to engage in the same process by learning a conceptualization of essential components of cooperative learning and their role in using formal and informal cooperative learning and cooperative base groups, and applying that conceptual model to their unique teaching situation, circumstances, students, and instructional needs. Each class may require a different adaption in order to maximize the effectiveness of cooperative learning.

Understanding the essential components allows teachers to think metacognitively about cooperative learning; create any number of lessons, strategies, and activities; take any lesson in any subject area and structure it cooperatively; practice and practice the use of cooperative learning until they are at a routine/integrated level of use and implement cooperative learning at least 60 percent of the time in their classrooms; describe precisely what they are doing and why they are doing it in order to communicate to others the nature of cooperative learning and teach colleagues how to implement cooperative learning in their classrooms and settings; and apply the principles of cooperation to other settings, such as collegial relationships and faculty meetings.

2. *Try out cooperative learning in the classroom.* Faculty members must be willing to take risks by experimenting with new instructional and management strategies and procedures. They risk short-term failure to gain long-term success in increasing their expertise. It must be assumed that efforts will fail to live up to expectations for a considerable length of time, during which the new strategy is overlearned to a routine-use, automatic level.

3. *Assess how well cooperative learning lessons are working and obtain feedback from others.* Although a lesson may not have gone well, from the progressive refinement point of view, failure never occurs. Efforts are simply approximations of what one wants and, with refining and fine-tuning of procedures and more practice, the approximations get successively closer and closer to the ideal.

4. *Reflect on what happened, make modifications, and try again.* The discrepancy between the real and the ideal guides plans for altering one's behavior to get a better match in the future. Using quality charts enhances this reflection process.

Perseverance in using cooperative learning is required until a teacher can teach a cooperative lesson routinely and without conscious planning or thought. With every lesson taught, a teacher's expertise in using cooperative learning is fine-tuned through this progressive refinement process.

Gaining and Sharing Expertise

Expertise is reflected in a person's proficiency, adroitness, competence, and skill. Cooperative efforts take more expertise than competitive or individualistic efforts because they involve dealing with other people as well as dealing with the demands of the task (i.e., simultaneously engaging in taskwork and teamwork). Expertise is usually gained in an incremental, step-by-step manner using the progressive refinement process in a team over a period of years.

Becoming adept in using cooperative learning in the classroom and cooperative teams in the school and district does not happen overnight. As we stated, with only a moderately difficult teaching strategy teachers may require from 20 to 30 hours of instruction in its theory, 15 to 20 demonstrations using it with different students and subjects, and an additional 10 to 15 coaching sessions to attain higher-level skills. For a more difficult teaching strategy such as cooperative learning, several years of training and support may be needed to ensure mastery. We prefer three years to train a teacher fully in the fundamentals of cooperative learning, the advanced use of cooperative learning, the use of academic controversies to encourage students within cooperative groups to challenge each other intellectually, and the use of a peer mediation system to ensure that students can negotiate constructive solutions to their own and classmates' conflicts. A similar sequence for administrators includes added training on leading the cooperative school.

Interested "cooperative learning superstars" can be trained to provide the three-year training program within their districts. During the training sessions teachers explore cooperative learning and the essential components that make it work. They then must transfer this knowledge to their own classrooms and maintain their use of cooperative learning. The success of training depends on transfer (teachers trying out cooperative learning in their classrooms) and maintenance (long-term use of cooperative learning). Transfer and maintenance, therefore, depend largely on teachers themselves being organized into collegial teaching teams that focus on helping each member become progressively more competent in using cooperative learning. There is no better way to learn how to use cooperative learning than to teach a colleague how to use it. As Harvey Firestone of Firestone Tires stated, "It is only when we develop others that we permanently succeed."

Quality of Implementation (Quality Charts)

Teachers must assess the quality of their efforts in implementing cooperative learning so they can continuously improve. Such assessment requires establishing a set of criteria and rating the extent to which each member of the collegial teaching team is meeting the criteria. The results can be charted each week to help the group determine the frequency and fidelity with which each member is implementing cooperative learning and set goals for implementation efforts for the coming week.

During the collegial teaching team meeting, members show their implementation logs and recount how they (1) taught at least one cooperative learning lesson per day, (2) planned a classroom routine to be done cooperatively, (3) taught at least one social skill, (4) assisted a colleague in using cooperative learning, (5) co-taught a lesson with a colleague, and (6) visited the classrooms of all other group members and noted something positive that was taking place. These criteria may be changed to make them more challenging according to group members' experience and competence level. More advanced criteria include using four types of positive interdependence in each lesson, conducting sequences of cooperative strategies within one lesson, and reading an article or chapter on cooperative learning.

Team members receive points according to the extent to which they reach each criterion (0 = did not do, 1 = half did, 2 = did). Thus, with this example, a group member could earn between 0 and 12 points per week. The points earned by team members are added together and divided by the number of members. The result is the team score, which is plotted on the group's *quality chart*. The team discusses the results and the long-term trend and plans how to either improve their implementation efforts during the coming week or maintain their high level of implementation.

Benchmarking

Benchmarking is establishing operating targets based on best known practices. When benchmarking, teachers identify "the best of the best" in instructional procedures. To study best practices in cooperative learning, educators must survey the research to see what has proven to be effective and locate the schools where the effective methods have been successfully implemented. After identifying "the best of the best," teachers set a goal to achieve that level of performance in their classes. The teachers must plan the methods they will use to achieve the goals without mimicking the past, and performance measures must be developed to evaluate every procedure's contribution toward reaching the established goals. The benchmark is moved higher as goals are reached.

Providing Leadership

Knowing is not enough; we must apply. Willing is not enough; we must do.

—Goethe

To implement the cooperative school, leadership must help faculty do a better job. Leaders can't spend their time in an office talking on the phone, writing memos, and putting out fires. They must spend their time "where the action is" (in Japan this is called *genba*). In schools, the action is in classrooms. Therefore, school leaders must support classroom teachers in their efforts to provide students with the best possible instruction. In general, such leadership is provided through five sets of actions (Johnson and Johnson 1989b):

(1) *Challenging the Status Quo.* The status quo is the competitive-individualistic, mass-production structure that now dominates schools and classrooms. In the classroom, it is represented by lecturing, whole-class discussion, individual worksheets, and tests on Friday. In the school, it is teachers and students separated into grade levels and academic departments with one teacher and one set of students per classroom. Leaders must challenge the efficacy of the status quo.

(2) *Inspiring a Mutual Vision of What the School Could and Should Be.* Good leaders enthusiastically and frequently communicate the vision of establishing the cooperative school. The leader is the keeper of

the dream who inspires commitment to the joint goal of creating a team-based, cooperative school.

(3) *Empowering Through Cooperative Teams.* This is the most important of all leadership activities. When faculty or students feel helpless and discouraged, providing them with a team creates hope and opportunity. Social support from, and accountability to, valued peers motivates committed efforts to achieve and succeed. Students are empowered by cooperative learning groups and faculty members are empowered through collegial teaching teams and involvement in site-based decision making.

(4) *Leading by Example.* Leaders model the use of cooperative strategies and procedures and take risks to increase their professional competence. Their actions must be congruent with their words. They must publicly demonstrate what they advocate.

(5) *Encouraging the Heart to Persist.* As we've said, long-term, committed efforts to continuously improve one's competencies come from the heart, not the head. It takes courage and hope to continue to strive for increased knowledge and expertise. Social support and concrete assistance from leaders and teammates provide students and educators with the strength needed to persist and excel.

Schools are not buildings, curriculums, and machines. Schools are relationships and interactions among people. How interpersonal interaction is structured determines schools' effectiveness. When teachers are seen as interchangeable parts in a machine created to mass-produce educated students, they tend to become isolated and alienated from each other and from their work. The benefits of cooperative teams, therefore, are great for faculty and students. A cooperative, team-based, high-performance school begins with the use of cooperative learning the majority of the time. It also involves collegial teaching teams, task forces, and ad hoc decision-making groups within the school. And because all schools reflect the systems within which they operate, administrative cooperative teams must be established at the district level.

A congruent organizational structure—one that promotes cooperation at all levels—ensures quality education by creating a constancy of purpose, a commitment to educating every student, a focus on improving the quality of instruction, the elimination of competition at all levels, strong personal relationships, a concern about reducing waste, and careful attention to successfully implementing cooperative learning to improve student achievement.

11

Final Thoughts: The Changing Paradigm of Teaching

Cooperative learning is part of a broader paradigm shift occurring in teaching. Figure 11.1 (see page 102) presents the essential elements of this paradigm shift (Johnson, Johnson, and Holubec 1992; Johnson, Johnson, and Smith 1991).

The old paradigm of teaching is based on John Locke's assumption that the untrained student mind is like a blank sheet of paper waiting for the instructor to write on it. Because of this and other assumptions, educators have often thought of teaching in terms of several principal activities:

- *Transferring knowledge from teacher to student.* The teacher's job is to give it; the student's job is to get it. Teachers transmit information that students are expected to memorize and then recall.

- *Filling passive, empty vessels with knowledge.* Students are passive recipients of knowledge. Teachers *own* the knowledge that students memorize and recall.

- *Classifying students* by deciding who gets which grade and sorting students into categories by deciding who does and doesn't meet the requirements to be graduated, go on to college, and get a good job. This is done based on the assumption that ability is fixed and unaffected by effort and education. Constant inspection is used to weed out "defective" students.

• *Conducting education within a context of impersonal relationships* among students and between teachers and students. Based on the Taylor model of industrial organizations, students and teachers are perceived to be interchangeable and replaceable parts in the "education machine."

• *Maintaining a competitive organizational structure* in which students work to outperform their classmates and teachers work to outperform their colleagues.

• *Assuming that anyone with expertise in a field can teach.* This is sometimes known as the content premise—if you have a Ph.D. in the field, you can teach regardless of whether or not you have any pedagogical training.

FIGURE 11.1
Comparison of Old and New Paradigms of Teaching

	Old Paradigm	New Paradigm
Knowledge	Transferred from Faculty to Students	Jointly Constructed by Students and Faculty
Students	Passive Vessels to be Filled by Faculty's Knowledge	Active Constructor, Discoverer, Transformer of Knowledge
Faculty Purpose	Classify and Sort Students	Develop Students' Competencies and Talents
Relationships	Impersonal Relationship Among Students and Between Faculty and Students	Personal Transaction Among Students and Between Faculty and Students
Context	Competitive/Individualistic	Cooperative Learning in Classroom and Cooperative Teams Among Faculty and Administrators
Assumption About Teaching	Any Expert Can Teach	Teaching Is Complex and Requires Considerable Training
Ways of Knowing	Logico-Scientific	Narrative
Epistemology	Reductionist	Constructivist
Mode of Learning	Memorization	Relating
Climate	Conformity/Cultural Uniformity	Diversity and Personal Esteem/ Cultural Diversity and Commonality

Source: D.W. Johnson, and K. Smith. (1991). *Active Learning.* Edina, Minn.: Interaction Book Company.

Thus, the old paradigm is to transfer teachers' knowledge to passive students so teachers can classify and sort students in a norm-referenced way through competition. Many teachers consider the old paradigm the only possibility. Lecturing while requiring students to be passive, silent, isolated, and in competition with each other seems the only way to teach. The old paradigm is carried forward by sheer momentum, while almost everyone persists in the hollow pretense that all is well. But all is not well.

Teaching is changing. The old paradigm is being dropped for a new paradigm based on theory and research with clear applications to instruction. Educators must now think of teaching in terms of several different principal activities.

• *Students construct, discover, transform, and extend their own knowledge.* Learning is something a learner does, not something that is done to a learner. Students do not passively accept knowledge from the teacher or curriculum. They use new information to activate their existing cognitive structures or construct new ones. The teacher's role in this activity is to create the conditions within which students can construct meaning from new material studied by processing it through existing cognitive structures and then retaining it in long-term memory where it remains open to further processing and possible reconstruction.

• *Teachers' efforts are aimed at developing students' competencies and talents.* Student effort should be inspired and secondary schools must "add value" by cultivating talent. A "cultivate and develop" philosophy must replace the "select and weed out" philosophy. Students' competencies and talents must be developed under the assumption that with effort and education, any student can improve.

• *Teachers and students work together, making education a personal transaction.* All education is a social process that can occur only through interpersonal interaction (real or implied). There is a general rule of instruction: The more pressure placed on students to achieve and the more difficult the material to be learned, the more important it is to provide social support within the learning situation. Challenge and social support must be balanced if students are to cope successfully with the stress inherent in learning situations. Learning results when individuals cooperate to construct shared understandings and knowledge. Teachers must be able to build positive relationships with students and create the conditions within which students build caring and committed relationships with each other. The school then becomes a learning community of committed scholars in the truest sense.

These activities can take place only within a cooperative context. When students interact within a competitive context, communication is minimized, misleading and false information is often communicated, assistance is viewed as cheating, and classmates and faculty tend to dislike and distrust each other. Competitive and individualistic learning situations, therefore, discourage active construction of knowledge and the development of talent by isolating students and creating negative relationships among classmates and teachers.

Classmates and teachers need to be seen as collaborators rather than as obstacles to students' own academic and personal success. Teachers, therefore, must structure learning situations so that students work together to maximize each other's achievement. Administrators, likewise, must create a cooperative, team-based organizational structure within which faculty work together to ensure each other's success (Johnson and Johnson 1989b).

Teaching is a complex application of theory and research that requires considerable teacher training and continuous refinement of skills and procedures. Becoming a good teacher takes at least one lifetime of continuous effort. Cooperative learning provides the means of operationalizing the new paradigm of teaching and provides the context that encourages the development of student talent. It's an important part of changing the passive and impersonal character of many classrooms. It ensures that students are cognitively, physically, emotionally, and psychologically involved in constructing their own knowledge and succeeding in school and life.

Creating a Learning Community

In *The Secret Garden*, Frances Hodgson Burnett states: "Where you tend a rose, a thistle cannot grow." Schools should tend roses. They can do so by creating a learning community characterized by cooperative efforts to achieve meaningful goals. In a recent review of research, Lisbeth Schorr concludes that caring is the most important attribute of effective schools. Education historians David Tyack and Elizabeth Hansot conclude that the theme running through all successful schools is that students, teachers, administrators, and parents share a sense of community and a "socially integrating sense of purpose."

A community is a limited number of people who share common goals and a common culture. The smaller the size of the community, the more personal the relationships, and the greater the personal accountability. Within communities, everyone knows everyone else. Relationships are long-term rather than temporary encounters. In learning communities instruction becomes personalized. Students are thought of as citizens, while teachers are thought of as community leaders. Thus, the learning community becomes an extended family where mutual achievement and caring for one another are important. With citizenship in such a community comes an ethical code that includes rules about students being prepared for classes each day, paying attention in class, being their personal best, and respecting other people and their property. Cooperative teams help create such learning communities.

Having read this book, you are now at a new beginning. Years of experience using cooperative learning are needed to gain the needed expertise. You will gain this expertise by implementing cooperative learning and helping others do so by being a contributing member of a collegial team, thus establishing a true learning community of scholars for both your students and yourself.

References

Aronson, E. (1978). *The Jigsaw Classroom*. Beverly Hills, Calif.: Sage Publications.

Astin, A., K. Green, W. Korn, and M. Shalit. (1986). *The American Freshman: Twenty Year Trends*. Los Angeles: University of California at Los Angeles, Higher Education Research Institute.

Blake, R., and J. Mouton. (1974). "Designing Change for Educational Institutions Through the D/D Matrix." *Educational and Urban Society* 6: 179-204.

Blumberg, A., J. May, and R. Perry. (1974). "An Inner-City School that Changed— and Continued to Change." *Education and Urban Society* 6: 222-238.

Campbell, J. (1965). "The Children's Crusader: Colonel Francis W. Parker." Doctoral dissertation, Columbia University.

Collins, B. (1970). *Social Psychology*. Reading, Mass.: Addison- Wesley.

Conger, J. (1988). "Hostages to Fortune: Youth, Values, and the Public Interest." *American Psychologist* 43: 291-300.

Dansereau, D. (1985). "Learning Strategy Research." In *Thinking and Learning Skills, Vol. 1: Relating Instruction to Research*, edited by J. Segal, S. Chipman, and R. Glaser. Hillsdale, N.J.: Lawrence Erlbaum Associates, Inc.

Deutsch, M. (1949a). "An Experimental Study of the Effects of Cooperation and Competition Upon Group Processes." *Human Relations* 2: 199-232.

Deutsch, M. (1949b). "A Theory of Cooperation and Competition." *Human Relations* 2: 129-152.

Deutsch, M. (1962). "Cooperation and Trust: Some Theoretical Notes." In *Nebraska Symposium on Motivation*, edited by M.R. Jones. Lincoln, Neb.: University of Nebraska Press.

DeVries, D., and K. Edwards. (1973). "Learning Games and Student Teams: Their Effects on Classroom Process." *American Educational Research Journal* 10: 307-318.

DeVries, D., and K. Edwards. (1974). "Student Teams and Learning Games: Their Effects on Cross-Race and Cross-Sex Interaction." *Journal of Educational Psychology* 66, 5: 741-749.

Dewey, J. (1924). *The School and Society*. Chicago: University of Chicago Press.

Harkins, S., and R. Petty. (1982). "The Effects of Task Difficulty and Task Uniqueness on Social Loafing." *Journal of Personality and Social Psychology* 43: 1214-1229.

Hill, G. (1982). "Group Versus Individual Performance: Are N + 1 Heads Better Than One?" *Psychology Bulletin* 91: 517-539.

Hwong, N., A. Caswell, D.W. Johnson, and R. Johnson. (in press). "Effects of Cooperative and Individualistic Learning on Prospective Elementary Teachers' Music Achievement and Attitudes. *Journal of Social Psychology*

Ingham, A., G. Levinger, J. Graves, and V. Peckham. (1974). "The Ringelmann Effect: Studies of Group Size and Group Performance." *Journal of Personality and Social Psychology* 10: 371-384.

Johnson, D.W. (1970). *The Social Psychology of Education*. New York: Holt, Rinehart & Winston.

Johnson, D.W. (1991). *Human Relations and Your Career*. Englewood Cliffs, N.J.: Prentice-Hall.

Johnson, D.W. (1993). *Reaching Out: Interpersonal Effectiveness and Self-Actualization* (5th ed.). Needham Heights, Mass.: Allyn and Bacon.

Johnson, D.W., and F. Johnson. (1991, 4th ed.; 1994, 5th ed.). *Joining Together: Group Theory and Group Skills* (5th ed.). Englewood Cliffs, N.J.: Prentice-Hall.

Johnson, D.W., and R. Johnson. (1974). "Instructional Goal Structure: Cooperative, Competitive, or Individualistic." *Review of Educational Research* 44: 213-240.

Johnson, D.W., and R. Johnson. (1977). "Controversy in the Classroom" (video). Edina, Minn.: Interaction Book Company.

Johnson, D.W., and R. Johnson. (1978). "Cooperative, Competitive, and Individualistic Learning. *Journal of Research and Development in Education* 12: 3-15.

Johnson, D.W., and R. Johnson. (1979). "Conflict in the Classroom: Controversy and Learning." *Review of Educational Research* 49: 51-70.

Johnson, D.W., and R. Johnson. (1983). "The Socialization and Achievement Crisis: Are Cooperative Learning Experiences the Solution?" In *Applied Social Psychology Annual* 4: 119-164.

Johnson, D.W., and R. Johnson. (1987). *Creative Conflict*. Edina, Minn.: Interaction Book Company.

Johnson, D.W., and R. Johnson. (1989). *Cooperation and Competition: Theory and Research*. Edina, Minn.: Interaction Book Company.

Johnson, D.W., and R. Johnson. (1975/1991a). *Learning Together and Alone: Cooperative, Competitive, and Individualistic Learning*. Englewood Cliffs, N.J.: Prentice-Hall.

Johnson, D.W., and R. Johnson. (1991b). *Teaching Students To Be Peacemakers*. Edina, Minn.: Interaction Book Company.

Johnson, D.W., and R. Johnson. (1991c). "Teaching Students To Be Peacemakers" (video). Edina, Minn. Interaction Book Company.

Johnson, D.W., and R. Johnson. (1991d). *My Mediation Notebook*. Edina, Minn.: Interaction Book Company.

Johnson, D.W., and R. Johnson. (1992a). *Creative Controversy: Intellectual Challenge in the Classroom*. Edina, Minn.: Interaction Book Company.

Johnson, D.W., and R. Johnson. (1992b). *Positive Interdependence: The Heart of Cooperative Learning*. Edina, Minn.: Interaction Book Company.

Johnson, D.W., and R. Johnson. (1992c). "Positive Interdependence: The Heart of Cooperative Learning." (video). Edina, Minn.: Interaction Book Company.

Johnson, D.W., and R. Johnson. (1994). *Leading the Cooperative School*. Edina, Minn.: Interaction Book Company.

Johnson, D.W., R.T. Johnson, and E. Holubec. (1993). *Cooperation in the Classroom (6th ed.)*. Edina, Minn.: Interaction Book Company.

Johnson, D.W., R.T. Johnson, and E. Holubec. (1992). *Advanced Cooperative Learning*. Edina, Minn.: Interaction Book Company.

Johnson, D.W., R. Johnson, A. Ortiz, and M. Stanne. (1991). "Impact of Positive Goal and Resource Interdependence on Achievement, Interaction, and Attitudes." *Journal of General Psychology* 118: 341-347.

Johnson, D.W., R. Johnson, and K. Smith. (1991). *Active Learning: Cooperation in the College Classroom*. Edina, Minn: Interaction Book Company.

Johnson, D.W., R. Johnson, M. Stanne, and A. Garibaldi. (1990). "The Impact of Leader and Member Group Processing on Achievement in Cooperative Groups." *The Journal of Social Psychology* 130: 507-516.

Kagan, S. (1988). *Cooperative Learning*. San Juan Capistrano, Calif.: Resources for Teachers.

Kerr, N. (1983). "The Dispensability of Member Effort and Group Motivation Losses: Freerider Effects." *Journal of Personality and Social Psychology* 44: 78-94.

Kerr, N., and S. Bruun. (1981). "Ringelmann Revisited: Alternative Explanations for the Social Loafing Effect." *Personality and Social Psychology Bulletin* 7: 224-231.

Kouzes, J., and B. Posner. (1987). *The Leadership Challenge*. San Francisco: Jossey-Bass.

Lamm, H., and G. Trommsdorff. (1973). "Group Verses Individual Performance on Tasks Requiring Ideational Proficiency (Brainstorming): A Review." *European Journal of Social Psychology* 3: 361-388.

Langer, E., and A. Benevento. (1978). "Self-Induced Dependence." *Journal of Personality and Social Psychology* 36: 886-893.

Latane, B., K. Williams, and S. Harkins. (1979). "Many Hands Make Light the Work: The Causes and Consequences of Social Loafing." *Journal of Personality and Social Psychology* 37: 822-832.

Lew, M., D. Mesch, D.W. Johnson, and R. Johnson. (1986a). "Positive Interdependence, Academic and Collaborative-Skills Group Contingencies and Isolated Students." *American Educational Research Journal* 23: 476-488.

Lew, M., D. Mesch, D.W. Johnson, and R. Johnson. (1986b). "Components of Cooperative Learning: Effects of Collaborative Skills and Academic Group Contingencies on Achievement and Mainstreaming." *Contemporary Educational Psychology* 11: 229-239.

Lewin, D. (1935). *A Dynamic Theory of Personality*. New York: McGraw-Hill.

Lewin, D. (1948). *Resolving Social Conflicts*. New York: Harper.

Little, J. (1987). "Teachers as Colleagues." In *Educator's Handbook: A Research Perspective*, edited by V. Koehler (pp. 491-518). New York: Longman.

Little, J. (1990). "The Persistence of Privacy: Autonomy and Initiative in Teachers' Professional Relations." *Teachers College Record* 9: 509-536.

Maller, J. (1929). *Cooperation and Competition: An Experimental Study in Motivation.* New York: Teachers College, Columbia University.

May, M, and L. Doob, (1937). "Competition and Cooperation." *Social Science Research Council Bulletin (No. 25).* New York: Social Science Research Council.

Mayer, A. (1903). "Uber Einzel Und Gesamtleistung Des Schul Kindes." *Archiv Fur Die Gesamte Psychologie* 1: 276-416.

Mesch, D., D.W. Johnson, and R. Johnson. (1988). "Impact of Positive Interdependence and Academic Group Contingencies on Achievement." *Journal of Social Psychology* 128: 345-352.

Mesch, D., M. Lew, D.W. Johnson, and R. Johnson. (1986). "Isolated Teenagers, Cooperative Learning and the Training of Social Skills." *Journal of Psychology* 120: 323-334.

Miller, L., and R. Hamblin. (1963). "Interdependence, Differential Rewarding, and Productivity." *American Sociological Review* 28: 768-778.

Moede, W. (1927). "Die Richtlinien Der Leistungs-Psychologie." *Industrielle Psychotechnik* 4: 193-207.

National Association of Secondary School Principals. (1984). *The Mood of American Youth.* Reston, Va.: Author.

Nias, J. (1984). "Learning and Acting the Role: Inschool Support for Primary Teachers." *Educational Review* 33: 181-190.

Pepitone, E. (1980). *Children in Cooperation and Competition.* Lexington, Mass.: Lexington Books.

Petty, R., S. Harkins, K. Williams, and B. Latane. (1977). "The Effects of Group Size on Cognitive Effort and Evaluation." *Personality and Social Psychology Bulletin* 3: 575-578.

Putnam, J., J. Rynders, D.W. Johnson, and R. Johnson. (1989). "Collaborative Skill Instruction for Promoting Positive Interactions Between Mentally Handicapped and Nonhandicapped Children." *Exceptional Children* 55: 550-557.

Rosenshine, B., and R. Stevens. (1986). "Teaching Functions." In *Handbook of Research on Teaching (3rd ed)*, edited by M.C. Wittrock. (pp. 376-391). New York: Macmillan.

Salomon, G. (1981). "Communication and Education: Social and Psychological Interactions." *People and Communication* 13: 9-271.

Seligman, M. (October 1988). "Boomer Blues." *Psychology Today* 22: 50-55.

Sharan, S., and R. Hertz-Lazarowitz. (1980). "A Group-Investigation Method of Cooperative Learning in the Classroom." Technical report, University of Tel Aviv, Israel.

Sheingold, K., J. Hawkins, and C. Char. (1984). "I'm the Thinkist, You're the Typist: The Interaction of Technology and the Social Life of Classrooms." *Journal of Social Issues* 40, 3: 49-60.

Slavin, R., (1980). "Cooperative Learning." *Review of Educational Research* 50: 315-342.

Slavin, R. (1985). "An Introduction to Cooperative Learning Research." In *Learning to Cooperate, Cooperating to Learn*, edited by R. Slavin, et al. New York: Plenum Press.

Slavin, R., M. Leavey, and N. Madden. (1982). *Team-Assisted Individualization: Mathematics Teacher's Manual.* Baltimore: Johns Hopkins University, Center for Social Organization of Schools.

Stevens, R., N. Madden., R. Slavin, and A. Farnish. (1987). "Cooperative Integrated Reading and Composition: Two Field Experiments." *Reading Research Quarterly* 22, 4: 433-454.

Triplett, N. (1988). "The Dynamogenic Factors in Pacemaking and Competition." *American Journal of Psychology* 9: 507-533.

Walton, M. (1986). *The Deming Management Method.* New York: Dood, Mead, and Company.

Webb, N., P. Ender, and S. Lewis. (1986). "Problem-Solving Strategies and Group Processes in Small Group Learning Computer Programming." *American Educational Research Journal* 23: 243-261.

Williams, K. (1981). "The Effects of Group Cohesiveness on Social Loafing." Paper presented at the annual meeting of the Midwestern Psychological Association, Detroit.

Williams, K., S. Harkins., and B. Latane. (1981). "Identifiability as a Deterrent to Social Loafing. Two Cheering Experiments." *Journal of Personality and Social Psychology* 40: 303-311.

Wilson, R. (1987). "Toward Excellence in Teaching." In *Techniques for Evaluating and Improving Instruction*, edited by L.M. Aleamoni, (pp. 9-24). San Francisco: Jossey-Bass.

Wittrock, M. (1990). "Generative Processes of Comprehension." *Educational Psychologist* 24: 345-376.

Yager, S., D. W. Johnson, and R. Johnson. (1985). "Oral Discussion, Group-To-Individual Transfer, and Achievement in Cooperative Learning Groups." *Journal of Educational Psychology* 77: 60-66.

Current ASCD Network

ASCD sponsors numerous Networks that help members exchange ideas, share common interests, identify and solve problems, grow professionally, and establish collegial relationships. The following Network may be of particular interest to readers of this book. For information about other Networks, call ASCD's Field Services Department at (703) 549-9110, ext. 506.

Cooperative Learning

Harlan Rimmerman, Director
N. Kansas City School District
2000 N.E. 46th Street
Kansas City, MO 64116
TEL: (816) 453-5050